The Prey of the Priest Catchers

The Lives of The 40 Martyrs

By Leo Knowles

THE PREY OF THE PRIEST CATCHERS
A Carillon Book
ISBN: 0-89310-057-9 (Hardcover)
0-89310-058-7 (Paperback)
Library of Congress Catalog Card Number 80-69148
Copyright © 1980 by Carillon Books
All rights reserved
Printed in the United States of America
CARILLON BOOKS is a division of
Catholic Digest
2115 Summit Ave.
St. Paul, Minnesota 55105
U.S.A.

Readers who would like a fuller account of the lives of Margaret Clitherow, Edmund Campion, and Philip Howard may care to turn to my book *Saints Who Spoke English* (Carillon Books, 1979).

L. K.

Contents

1
The Storm Breaks

Most visitors to London will know Marble Arch, the magnificent gateway which once served as an entrance to Hyde Park but which now stands in isolation, cut off from the park's green acres by the traffic which swirls round it. A stone's throw away are the stores of Oxford Street and the hotels of Park Lane, the tower of the London Hilton rising high over the trees. Just inside the park itself is Speaker's Corner, home of the open-air orators, a magnet for Londoners and tourists alike, where the biggest and liveliest audience is often the one round the crucifix of the Catholic Evidence Guild.

Occasionally a visitor may be seen, apparently oblivious of all this teeming life, standing on the sidewalk at the busy intersection and peering among the traffic as though for some lost object. Soon he sees what he is looking for: a triangular brass plate set in the roadway a few yards northwest of the arch's graceful bulk.

The plate marks the site of Tyburn, for 600 years the

bloodiest spot in England, where thieves and murderers, forgers and traitors paid the penalty for their crimes, and where no fewer than 90 martyrs gave their lives for the Catholic faith.

In the days of Henry VIII Tyburn stood, as it stands today, on rising ground at the junction of four main roads. Then, however, it was in the countryside, surrounded by green fields and trees. Close by ran the stream—a tributary of the Thames—which gave the gallows its name. "Tyburn Tree" the Tudor crowds called it, as they hurried from the city to enjoy the spectacle of some poor wretch being tortured to death in public.

On a May morning in 1535 the audience assembled as usual before the Tyburn gallows, but this time the gala atmosphere was missing. People walked more slowly, did not exchange jokes, talked in subdued voices. How was it possible, they asked each other, that five priests who had done no harm, who were much loved and renowned for their holiness and learning, could be dragged here to be hanged, drawn, and quartered like criminals?

The condemned men had, meanwhile, already set out on their terrible three-mile journey from the Tower of London. As they were led from their cells and lay down on the wattled hurdles, Thomas More and his daughter, Margaret, watched through the bars of Thomas's own cell.

"Dost thou not see, Meg," observed Thomas, "that these blessed Fathers be now going to their deaths as bridegrooms to a marriage?" It was their life of self-sacrifice and prayer, he told her, which had won for them the grace to accept martyrdom with joy.

Out through the great gate and down Tower Hill the slow procession moved, into the city where on either side of the narrow streets silent crowds waited, horrified and yet fascinated by the sight which they were to see.

A heavy, eerie scraping sound, echoing between the tightly packed houses, told the watchers that the procession was near. Another moment and they could see the armed guards and then the horses pulling the condemned men to their deaths.

Three hurdles were dragged over the rough London cobblestones on that Tuesday morning nearly 450 years ago. On the first, two priests were tied together, on the second two more. The fifth priest was tied alone on the remaining hurdle.

As the crowd got its first glimpse of them a gasp ran along its ranks. By the king's special order the four Religious had been tied to the hurdles wearing their Religious habits, a thing never before seen in England.

Three of the victims—John Houghton, Augustine Webster and Robert Lawrence—were Carthusians, each the prior of a different Charterhouse. Richard Reynolds was a member of the Bridgettine Order and John Haile was a secular priest aged almost 80.

Feet up behind the horses' tails, heads only an inch from the ground, the five priests bumped and scraped their way towards Tyburn. Through mud, puddles, rotting garbage and horse dung the horses dragged them until the white Carthusian habits were, like the victims' faces, covered in filth.

Halfway along the route the procession stopped and the condemned men were offered a bowl of ale. As the hurdles were raised and the drink held to their lips, a woman stepped forward from the crowd and wiped the bespattered faces. She asked and received a blessing, and the procession moved on.

We do not know in what order the five were dragged to Tyburn, but it is probable that John Houghton, prior

of the London Charterhouse, was one of the pair on
the first hurdle, for we know that he was the first to
die. Besides, King Henry and his chief secretary,
Thomas Cromwell, must have wanted the crowds to
take a good look at this renowned confessor and
spiritual director, head of one of the greatest of London monasteries, as he paid the penalty for his loyalty
to Rome.

When news of the king's "Great Matter"—his efforts
to gain a divorce from Catherine of Aragon—first
penetrated the monastery walls, Prior John and his
monks must have thought that it could have little to do
with them. They lived, as Carthusians still live today,
in strict seclusion from the world, a community of
hermits, each spending much of his time in a "cell"
which was in effect a tiny cottage, with its own workroom, bedroom, oratory, and garden.

This was the life which their founder, the German
St. Bruno, had adopted with his companions when
they settled near Grenoble in the French Alps late in
the 11th century. Their house became known as the
Grand Chartreuse and when the Order reached England, "Chartreuse" was anglicized into "Charterhouse."

When John came to the London Charterhouse in
1515 he was already a priest, ordained four years
previously at the age of 24. Son of an Essex family, he
had taken a law degree at Cambridge University and
was destined by his parents for a worldly career and a
prosperous marriage. Knowing that he was called to
the priesthood, John ran away from home and lived
with a local pastor while he studied theology. Tal-
ented and strong willed, he might have risen to high
office in the Church. He had not been a secular priest
for long, however, when he realized that it was not in
the parish ministry but in a contemplative Order that
his vocation lay.

In offering himself to the Carthusians John chose what was then, and is today, widely admitted to be an exceptionally tough form of monastic life—some would say the toughest. Of all monastic Orders, the Carthusians alone have never departed from the strictness of their original Rule and have never needed reform.

Apart from the solitude, which requires great psychological strength, Carthusians impose many bodily penances on themselves. They remain strict vegetarians and fast frequently on bread and water. Their two short periods of sleep are broken each night by four hours of Office in choir and private prayer in their cells.

This austere Order has always tested candidates strictly before allowing them to take vows. When he arrived at the London Charterhouse, therefore, young Father John was not shown straight to a cell but lodged for a time in the guesthouse.

Here he was visited by the prior, a saintly Irishman named William Tynbygh, of whom a remarkable story was told—one which John must surely have heard. As a young man of 20 William was travelling in the Holy Land when Saracens captured him and sentenced him to death. Praying for deliverance, he fell asleep and awoke, safe and sound, in his own bed at home in Ireland! His family, naturally overjoyed, made such a fuss about the miracle that William fled to London and the security of the Charterhouse.

Whether miraculously rescued or not, William was a man of outstanding spiritual gifts, worthy to train a future saint. He swiftly recognized John's genuine Carthusian vocation and, when the brethren had voted their agreement, clothed him in the habit of a novice.

It was now that John found himself in a cell of his own, alone with God between those four narrow walls.

An elderly monk came to show him the use of the few carpentry tools in his workroom and how to tend his tiny garden. In a Carthusian monastery, as in others, manual labor is part of every monk's day. Other monks taught him to sing the Office in the Carthusian manner—very slowly—and to celebrate Mass in the Order's own rite.

At night, when the bell rang, the novice would leave his cell and join his brethren in the Great Cloister. From there they would walk in procession to the church, filing into choir for the long night Office.

How romantic it must all have seemed at first to the earnest young priests, especially that night procession, the lantern casting long shadows on the wall of the cloister as the white-robed monks filed solemnly into the church!

The testing time would come, of course, when the novelty had worn off and when the bed in his cell, though hard, seemed infinitely more attractive than the cold stones of the cloister and the great, unheated choir, when the psalms of the Office ceased to seem beautiful but became monotonous, and when the hours of chanting dragged by on leaden feet. In the daytime, too, there would be periods of dryness when God seemed far away and the cell a wearisome prison.

We can be sure that John did not escape such trials; later on he showed great sympathy towards others who suffered them. Yet he triumphed and became not only a fully professed Carthusian but one whose qualities marked him out as a future leader and teacher. After seven years he was appointed sacristan, a post of particular importance in a monastery famed for the dignity and reverence of its worship.

Although the monks guarded their solitude carefully it was inevitable that the London Charterhouse should exercise a very real influence on the world outside.

Founded by a pious French knight after the plague of 1368, it stood at first on the edge of the capital beside a cemetery where plague victims were buried. Here the first 12 monks prayed for the souls of these poor Londoners who, all too often, had no relative left to pray for them. During the next century and a half the monastery expanded its property greatly, thanks to legacies and other gifts, so that by the time John arrived its fields and orchards stretched over 13 acres, running up among the town houses of the great. Awed and curious citizens would gaze across the monastic lands as the white-robed figures in the distance took the weekly walk in the open air which their Rule prescribed.

Yet those who sought the monks' help found the kindest of welcomes, for the monks had withdrawn from the world not in order to hate it but to love it more. The poor were given alms, the distressed consoled, the conscience-stricken absolved.

Here, before John's time, came the young Thomas More, then at the beginning of his legal career. Thomas stayed at the Charterhouse for four years, following his profession while discovering whether or not he had a Carthusian vocation. Even as a twice-married husband and the father of a family he had a Carthusian confessor and it seems that he dreamed of reentering the Charterhouse in his declining years. If King Henry and Cromwell thought to frighten Thomas by allowing him to see John and his brethren dragged off to Tyburn, they could have made no greater mistake. Their deaths encouraged him on his own road to martyrdom.

It was the procurator of the monastery who saw to the welfare of guests like Thomas. When, after another five years, John Houghton was appointed to this post he was much dismayed, for the procurator was responsible for all dealings with the outside world and he feared that his own inner life would suffer. In fact it did not, for the Order in its wisdom also gives the procurator the spiritual care of the lay brothers and so ensures that he does not become too distracted by worldly business.

In 1530 John was elected prior of the Charterhouse at Beauvale, in Nottinghamshire. No doubt he found it a wrench to leave the London house where he had spent so many years and the brethren whom he loved so much. But he accepted the promotion as God's will and set out on the journey north.

He had been at Beauvale for a bare six months when the prior of the London Charterhouse, Dom John Batmanson, died after reigning for only two years. By a unanimous vote the London monks reclaimed John Houghton to be their new prior.

In the world outside black storm clouds were gathering rapidly. For several years Henry VIII had been badgering Pope Clement to grant him a divorce from Queen Catherine and bullying the English bishops into giving him their support. In February, 1531, with no divorce forthcoming, Henry had Parliament proclaim him head of the Church in England "as far as the law of God permits"—a clause inserted into the Act to salve episcopal consciences.

At this time of danger and perplexity John took over as prior in London, realizing fully that if the Church was threatened, the monks' prayers were needed all the more and that they must reach new and greater heights of holiness.

For much of what we know about his rule we are indebted to one of his young monks, Maurice Chauncy, who lacked the courage to face martyrdom but made sure by his writings that his martyred brethren would be remembered. After taking the oath of supremacy Maurice escaped with other monks to Belgium, where he lived until Queen Mary ascended the throne and England became, for a few years, Catholic once more.

John was, he tells us, "short, modest, graceful, venerable, winning." With young monks he would seem reserved and somewhat stern, though with older ones he was tactful and easy to approach.

Visiting a brother in his cell, John would announce that he had left the office of prior at the door. "Here I am your friend, your brother," he would say, "you may speak to me freely."

Compliments, effusiveness, and obsequious behavior caused him embarrassment and distress. "It is not lawful for a poor Carthusian monk to broaden the fringes of his garment, or to be called by all men Rabbi," he protested.

He would ask after the brother's health, his family, how he spent his time, what were his favorite devotions. If he was suffering a period of dryness, John would assure him that this was God's way of testing him.

On the other hand, he was insistent that all ceremonial marks of respect due to the prior should be properly paid, since they were part of the Rule and belonged to the office, not the man.

Above all John demanded that the worship of God should be carried out with all the care and dignity of which human beings were capable. Once, during the long night Office, he walked out because the tired monks were singing too faintly. On another night, when they made a mistake in a psalm, he reminded them that they were singing with the angels, who never went wrong. Pomposity in reading, too, was firmly checked. "The wish to seem learned springs from pride," he would remind the offender gently.

With the angry or disobedient John was no less firm and no less gentle. "If you were in the world, good brother, you ought not to follow your own inclination in all things," he would say, urging the erring monk to do penance. Older offenders were reminded that the youngsters were watching them.

One dreadful day a monk who was possibly deranged attacked the prior physically. As the shocked brethren looked on John knelt and, quite literally, turned the other cheek. When the monk raised his fists to strike more blows, the others moved in and would have handled him roughly, but John commanded them to leave him alone. By way of punishment he simply ordered the monk confined to his cell for a few days as an example to others.

On January 25, 1533, King Henry went through a form of marriage secretly with a pregnant Anne Boleyn. On May 23, Thomas Cranmer, the newly appointed Archbishop of Canterbury, declared the king's marriage to Catherine null and void.

Returning from choir one night, John and his monks saw a comet hanging over their monastery, its rays flashing and sparkling through the branches of a tall tree. The rays seemed to fall and strike the belfry of their church. A few days later the walls of the Charterhouse were covered with a plague of dirty black flies, and soon afterwards with insects like dragon flies of various sizes.

Looking at each other the monks asked what these signs could mean. To John they meant only one thing: that the brethren must pray more fervently than ever before.

"God give grace, son, that these matters within a while be not confirmed with oaths," a worried Thomas More had confided to his son-in-law, William Roper.

Nobody knew the king better than his former lord chancellor, and Thomas's fears proved only too real.

On May 4, 1534, commissioners arrived at the Charterhouse to administer the oath of succession to the monks. Thomas had already refused to take the oath, which required all citizens to acknowledge Henry's first marriage as void and his union with Anne Boleyn as lawful. It also repudiated the rights of "any foreign authority, prince, or potentate."

John pleaded that he and his brethren should not have to take the oath since it was no part of their vocation as monks to interfere in royal affairs. "It does not concern me whom the king is pleased to accept or reject as his wife," he added.

This reply was hardly acceptable. The king and Cromwell were well aware of the monks' influence on those who came to them for guidance and were for that reason particularly determined to have their acquiescence. When the commissioners demanded a plain statement of the prior's attitude to the marriage, John looked them straight in the eye. "I cannot understand," he said, "how a marriage, celebrated according to the rites of the Church and observed for so long, can be made void."

It was a bold reply. England's former lord chancellor, the king's friend, was already in the Tower for saying less. Now John and his procurator, Humphrey Littlemore, were taken to the grim fortress by the Thames. There they were kept in appalling conditions. When they asked if these might be alleviated, they were told that if they complained they would lose what little they had.

Soon they had important visitors. John Stokesley, Bishop of London, and Edward Lee, Archbishop of York, came to persuade them to give way. No article of faith was, they assured the monks, involved in the issue of the succession to the throne. It was not a matter on which they ought to sacrifice their lives. Humble and obedient by training, the two monks took the oath.

If this seems shocking, or at least surprising, we should remember that the validity of the king's marriage was a more complicated question than it appears to us. Catherine had previously been betrothed to the king's brother and the marriage only went ahead after some hesitation on Henry's part. Two passages in the Book of Leviticus seemed to indicate that it might be invalid and even John Fisher, a considerable theologian, took two years to make up his mind about the case. Now Bishop John, too, was a prisoner in the Tower, soon to be martyred and eventually canonized.

Back home at the Charterhouse John Houghton confided to his brethren that during his imprisonment he had dreamed that he would shortly return to the Tower. "There remains, I think—though faith is not to be given to dreams—something else that shall be proposed to us," he explained gravely.

He was right. Rome declared Catherine's marriage valid and excommunicated Henry. On February 1, 1535, a new Act of Parliament made it high treason for any subject to deny that the king was the sole and supreme head of the Church in England.

Knowing what was to come, the monks prepared themselves with a solemn triduum of prayer. On the first day each made a general confession of his sins. On the second there was a general chapter at which each asked and received the forgiveness of his brethren for past faults. On the third, John celebrated a conventual Mass of the Holy Spirit.

Immediately after the Elevation the adoring monks felt a gentle breeze sweep over them—no ordinary breeze, but one which touched each one inwardly at the same time. To some its sound seemed like an echoing harmony. These brave men, so many of them soon to be martyred, had felt the presence of the Spirit whose help they sought. It was some time before John, who was in tears, could continue the Mass.

The monks had declared their readiness to die rather than acknowledge the king's supremacy. John was convinced that the choice would not be offered to all of them.

"Many of you are of noble blood," he said, "and what they will do is this: me and the elder brethren they will kill, and they will dismiss you that are young into a world which is not for you. If, therefore, it depend on me alone—if my oath will suffice—I will throw myself for your sakes on the mercy of God. I will make myself anathema and, to preserve you from these dangers, I will consent to the king's will.

"If, however, they have determined otherwise—if they choose to have the consent of all—the will of God be done. If one death will not avail, we will die all."

In order to keep his community together, in order that the vocation of the young monks should not be sacrificed, John Houghton was actually prepared to risk his own soul by taking the oath with a mental reservation. This, surely, was a sacrifice more terrible than martyrdom itself. In the end God did not ask it of him.

As soon as the new law came into force Cromwell's henchmen set out on their tour of Religious houses, demanding that those within swear on the Gospels their acceptance of the king's supremacy. This time there was to be no conscience-easing clause. Submission must be total and unconditional.

John decided not to wait until they came hammering on the door of the Charterhouse. Instead he would go to Thomas Cromwell, tell him that the oath in its present form offended the monks' consciences, and see whether any compromise could be found.

How little John knew the king's chief secretary! Cromwell was the kind of scheming, ruthless bureaucrat found today in many a totalitarian state or business corporation. Son of a brewer and blacksmith, he had served as a soldier and worked for commercial firms in Florence and Antwerp before returning to London. There he entered Cardinal Wolsey's service, trained as a lawyer and, when the cardinal fell from grace, adroitly switched to the king's personal staff, where his energy and efficiency swiftly brought him to the top.

Newly promoted, Cromwell was naturally anxious to please. Besides, Wolsey's fate had showed him what happened to royal officials who did not achieve what the king expected of them. When the cardinal failed to obtain the longed for divorce only his timely death saved him from the block.

In the end Cromwell was indeed destined to displease his royal master and to pay for it with his head. As John was shown into his office, however, he was the second most powerful man in England; to him Henry had given the task of bringing the Church under the king's heel.

They faced each other, the gentle monk dressed in his simple habit, and the squat, heavy-jowled tyrant in his furs and velvets, staring across the desk from hard, passionless eyes. Beside John stood his fellow priors, Augustine and Robert, who had come to London to seek his advice in the danger that threatened them.

The interview did not last long. As soon as he realized their purpose, Cromwell refused to discuss their position and ordered them to return to the Charterhouse until they were sent for.

The summons came the very next day. This time
Cromwell was flanked by Sir Thomas Audley, now
lord chancellor of England in place of the deposed
Thomas More and the man who was soon to pass
sentence on his old friend. On the other side sat two
ecclesiastics, Dr. Tregunnell and Thomas Bedyll,
Archdeacon of Cornwall, one of the royal commissioners who had once come to the Charterhouse to
administer the oath.

Humbly John begged that, since the monks could
not take the oath with a good conscience, they might
be exempted from it. "For," he asked, "what have we
poor monks to do with the decrees of princes, or how
can your laws concern us?"

If John had entertained any hopes of moving
Cromwell, they were dashed now. Since all the king's
subjects, clerical and lay, had consented to the Act of
Supremacy, declared the chief secretary, by their
refusal the Carthusians were setting themselves up as
wiser and holier than the rest of the nation. Warning
them that they would find themselves in serious
trouble if they persisted, he sent them home once
more to think over their position.

Three days later, on April 20, they were summoned
again. This time John attempted to prove the Pope's
supremacy from Scripture. If Christ gave the keys to
Peter, he argued, how could a king claim to hold
them?

Once more the interview was cut short. This time
three monks were taken to the Tower, though Augustine and Robert had not opened their lips. The journey
was by boat and they entered by Traitor's Gate.

Though John had been imprisoned there before, for
his companions this was their first—and last—visit.
Robert had originally been a London monk, and when
John was so quickly called back from Beauvale, he had

gone there as prior in his stead. Before going to Lincolnshire Augustine had belonged to the Charterhouse of Sheen, in Surrey, largest of the nine Carthusian monasteries in pre-Reformation England. Like John he was a Cambridge graduate.

In another dungeon sat Richard Reynolds, who had been taken from his cell at Syon Abbey in Middlesex when Henry's commissioners failed to extract the desired response. Richard, another Cambridge man, had joined the Bridgettine Order after a distinguished academic career and was reputed to be the most learned monk in England, the only one versed in Latin, Greek and Hebrew. Since Richard was equally well know for his holiness, it would be a triumph indeed if he could be made to take the oath, for then many troubled consciences would be eased.

Syon Abbey, to which he belonged, was a double community of nuns and monks, the only one in England belonging to the Order founded by St. Bridget, the saint and visionary who was queen of Sweden. To Syon came many troubled souls; not long before, John Houghton himself had sought advice there and had been told by a much-respected monk, "Better to die than recognize the king as head of the Church." Ironically, that same monk, John Fewterer, failed when his turn came. He took the oath of supremacy.

On April 26 Cromwell and his advisers came to the Tower and again urged the prisoners to give way.

"Kings are by divine right superior to priests, bishops and the Pope himself," he declared, quoting the Old Testament cases of David, Solomon, Ezechias and Cyrus in support of his claim.

"But the Roman Church has always taught to the contrary," declared the prisoners. They would stand firm in the Catholic faith, which could not be contrary to divine law, and they would accept the king's supremacy only so far as divine law allowed.

"I will have no conditions," roared Cromwell, "I care nothing what the Church has believed or taught."

"The supremacy of the Pope is necessary for salvation," insisted John Houghton, "instituted by Christ for the conservation of the Church."

"What care I for the Church?" Cromwell stormed. "Will you consent or will you not?"

"Disobey the Church? Renounce the Church? Never!" was John's reply.

The record of this interrogation, still preserved in London's Public Record Office, shows that the other two Carthusians showed no less spirit:

> "Robert Lawrence says there is one Catholic Church of which the Bishop of Rome is the head, therefore he cannot believe that the king is supreme head of the Church. . . . Augustine Webster says that he cannot take the king to be supreme head of the Church, but him that is by the doctors of the Church taken as head of the Church, that is, the Bishop of Rome."

A Protestant commentator noted darkly, "In this blindness, their superstitious minds were stabled."

On April 29 the four Religious were tried in Westminster Hall and accused of "treacherously machinating to deprive the king of his title of supreme head of the Church of England." This was nonsense, for they had machinated against no one; they had asked only to be left in peace.

John Haile, who stood beside them in the dock, faced the somewhat different charge of seditious conversation and criticism of the king's second marriage. The village of Isleworth, where John was pastor, included Syon Abbey, so John and Richard Reynolds must have known each other well. The parish was well known to be a hotbed of Catholic feeling. By putting the aged pastor on trial, Cromwell no doubt hoped to strike terror into his flock.

The prisoners made no defense, beyond denying that they had shown malice towards the king. Audley, the lord chancellor, asked Richard why he persisted in an opinion condemned by the judgment of so many lords and bishops and of the whole of Parliament.

The Bridgettine replied that he had intended to keep silence like our Lord, but that he would now speak in discharge of his own conscience and those of others.

"I have all the rest of Christendom in my favor," he declared. "I can even say that I have all this kingdom in my favor, although the smaller part holds with you; for I am sure that the larger part is at heart of my opinion, although outwardly, partly from fear and partly from hope, they profess to be of yours."

By this time his judges must have been red with anger, but Richard pressed on. He had dead witnesses, too, on his side: all the general councils, all historians and all the doctors of the Church for the last 1500 years.

At this point the judges had heard enough. Audley, regretting bitterly the opportunity which he had provided, brusquely ordered Richard to hold his tongue.

"Well then," he replied mildly, "judge me according to your law."

The jury was reluctant to convict and bravely tried to avoid bringing in the required verdict. They gave way only when Cromwell in person stormed into the jury room and warned them that they, too, might suffer the fate of traitors if they failed to find the prisoners guilty.

At Tyburn a large collection of noblemen waited to

see the butchery. Five of them were masked and a rumor swept through London that behind one of the masks was the king himself. In fact, Henry was not there. Though he would doubtless have liked to see his victims die, he stayed at home eagerly awaiting the news that all was over.

When the executioner knelt and asked his victims for the customary pardon, John Houghton embraced him. In a firm voice he called on the crowd to witness that he had refused to obey the king, not from malice, but solely for fear of offending God.

"Our holy mother the Church has decreed and enjoined otherwise than the king and Parliament have decreed," he declared. "I am therefore bound in conscience, and am ready and willing to suffer every kind of torture rather than deny a doctrine of the Church."

He asked his hearers to pray for him and for his brethren. As he commended his soul to God, the cart was driven from under him.

The executioners used a specially thick rope for fear he might die before he was cut down and the disembowelling began. As the executioner groped deep inside him, John, still conscious, knew what was happening. "Good Jesus, what will You do with my heart?" he murmured.

A moment later the heart was torn from his body and he was dead.

Each of the martyrs, as he mounted the cart, was offered a free pardon if he would renounce the Pope's supremacy. Each refused. Augustine and Robert preached to the bystanders, urging them to obey the king in all that was not against the honor of God and his Church.

The last to die was Richard Reynolds. While the others suffered he encouraged them constantly, promising them a heavenly supper to follow their sharp breakfast taken patiently for their Master's sake. Then he, too, preached a powerful sermon to the crowd. An eyewitness reported, "He never changed color nor was disquieted, and then in the end lastly went to die manfully himself."

When all was over, portions of the hacked-up bodies were put on view in public places all over London. John Houghton's arm was exhibited outside his own monastery, on an archway which may still be seen.

The king was very angry when he heard of the deep impression which the monks' farewell addresses had made upon the public. Their brethren, Henry resolved, must at all costs be made to submit.

Most of the Syon monks did so, but the Carthusians proved much harder to break. On the very day of the execution, commissioners went to the Charterhouse and interviewed the three monks who had taken over its government: Humphrey Middlemore, who had been John's companion during his first spell in the Tower; William Exmew, the dead prior's confessor; and Sebastian Newdigate, who had left the gaiety of King Henry's court to follow his monastic vocation.

Their answers proving unsatisfactory, the monks were shortly afterwards taken to the Marshalsea prison, where they were kept chained to columns for two weeks. During this time Sebastian had a visitor. King Henry came in disguise to try to persuade his ex-courtier to give way. Sebastian refused.

On June 12 he and his two companions were tried on the same trumped-up charge of treason which had been used against their brethren. One week later they, too, died at Tyburn.

From that moment onwards the remaining Carthusians "never knew what it was to be free from vexation for a single hour." A Sheen monk who had taken the oath of supremacy was placed over them as prior and he in turn was supervised by lay commissioners who lived in the monastery.

Monks thought to be especially loyal to the Pope were sent elsewhere. Two of these, John Rochester and William Walworth, found themselves in the Charterhouse at Hull, from which one of them sent an imprudent letter to the duke of Norfolk. As a result both were tried at York and executed on May 11, 1537.

Meanwhile Henry's commissioners were increasing the pressure on the London monks. When they threatened to suppress the Charterhouse out of hand, 19 of the exhausted monks gave way and took the oath of supremacy, hoping that by doing so they would at least save the monastery from destruction.

Of the ten who stood firm Thomas Johnson, Richard Beer, and Thomas Green were priests; John Davy a deacon; and Robert Salt, William Greenwood, Thomas Reding, Thomas Scryven, Walter Pierson, and William Horn, lay brothers. All were promptly taken to a filthy dungeon in Newgate.

Henry now realized his mistake in executing his previous victims in public. Their courage and dignity had only excited the sympathy and admiration of the crowd—the last reaction he desired.

The ten Carthusians were, therefore, neither charged nor tried. Instead they were tied to pillars, just as their brethren had been, and there they were left, starving and covered in filth, to die by slow degrees.

To the stinking dungeon one day came a young woman dressed as a milkmaid. She swiftly cleaned up the helpless men and fed them from her basket of food. Her name was Margaret Clement.

As a young girl she had been adopted by Thomas More as a companion for his own daughter. Now married and the mother of a young family, she risked her own life to help Thomas's friends. By bribing the jailer she was able to visit the monks until the king expressed surprise that they were still alive.

Terrified that Henry would discover what he had done, the jailer refused to allow Margaret into the prison. One by one the monks died, until only the lay brother William Horn was left alive.

For reasons never made clear, William was taken from the dungeon to the Tower, where his treatment was less cruel. Perhaps the submission of so firm a soul would have given Henry particular satisfaction, and it may have been that hope which made Henry keep the Carthusian alive for another three years.

William remained firm, however, and was finally brought to trial. He died at Tyburn on August 4, 1540, the last of the Carthusian martyrs.

In this chapter we have met only some of the brave men who faced the anger of Henry VIII rather than betray the Pope. There is not space to tell of John Forrest, the Fransiscan burned for "heresy," of his brother Franciscan Anthony Browne, of the Doncaster Carmelite Laurence Cooke, or of others like them up and down the land.

I will mention John Stone, an Augustinian friar at Canterbury, the ancient town where St. Augustine had settled when St. Gregory the Great sent him to England more than a thousand years before. John was a Doctor of Divinity, and much renowned for his holiness and learning.

When the king's visitor arrived John showed so much spirit in refusing to take the oath that they ordered him to be kept in solitary confinement within the priory for a year, in the hope of breaking his spirit. At the end of the year the visitor had to report that

John Stone "still held and still desired to die for it, that the king may not be head of the Church in England."

Thus Cromwell had him thrown into jail, where he added voluntary penances to the sufferings inflicted upon him. After fasting for three days he heard a voice call him by name and urge him to be of good courage and not to hesitate to suffer for the truth which he had professed.

He was executed on a high mound in Canterbury on a December day in 1539. The bill for the expenses of the execution, still preserved there, includes this item: "For a halter to hang him, one penny."

By this time many of England's monasteries had been pillaged and the great London Charterhouse was no more. Its monks had been dispersed, its books seized, and its trees, stones, and glass carted away by the ton to enrich the royal residence at Chelsea. Mass was still celebrated in the churches, folk still received the sacraments, and the outward forms of religion remained unchanged. Yet, as they saw the monasteries destroyed before their eyes, many an English man and woman must have realized, however dimly, that their country was Catholic no more.

2

Come Rack, Come Rope

It was a bright June day, with the white clouds sailing gently over the rocky Cornish landscape and no hint of disaster in the air. On Mr. Francis Tregian's estate at Golden the various employees went about their tasks as usual, the farmhands sweating in the fields, the maids rubbing and polishing indoors.

Cuthbert, the squire's steward, seemed to have little work to do, for he walked quietly up and down the garden, apparently absorbed in his own thoughts, his lips moving as though in prayer. Cuthbert, indeed, generally did little work about the estate and was often away. Yet nobody ever spoke to him about it, and his employer clearly thought a great deal of the grave, gently spoken servant who had joined the household a year before.

Outside in the fields, a thunder of hooves made the farm hands straighten up from their tasks and stare anxiously towards the road beyond the estate. Suddenly the horsemen were in sight—a hundred of them, armed and scowling. At their head was a man everyone recognized at once. Richard Grenville, sheriff of Cornwall, was a fanatical Protestant, known for his hatred of Rome and of all who held fast to the old religion.

"See the fear in their papist faces," muttered Grenville to his nearest henchman, his sharp eyes darting sideways. "They know on what errand we have come."

Up the drive to the house they rode, while the workers looked at each other mutely. At the door Francis Tregian, a middle-aged dignified man in sober dress, bowed courteously as the sheriff reigned his horse abruptly.

"To what do I owe this honor, Sir Richard?" he asked.

Coldly Grenville stared down at the squire. Tregian, he well knew, was a Catholic and an active one. His men had been watching the house for a long time.

"I have reason to believe that there lies here one Bourne, a known criminal wanted for felony in London," he announced. "My men and I have come to arrest him."

Tregian's gaze was calm and steady.

"I know nobody of that name," he replied, "and I harbor no criminal within my house."

"Do you say so, Master Tregian?" asked Grenville sneeringly. "Well then, you will make no objection if we look for ourselves—simply in order to be sure."

Francis Tregian drew himself up and returned the sheriff's stare without flinching.

"On the contrary," he said, "I should think it a great discourtesy for any one of you to enter my home for such a purpose, especially as I am a gentleman and you have no warrant."

Dismounting from his horse, Grenville thrust his coarse face into Tregian's.

"If I may not go in with your permission, then by heaven I shall do so without it," he roared, his hand on the dagger in his belt. Tregian's protests were drowned as the sheriff thrust him aside and stamped into the house followed by his men.

On the ground floor they threw open doors, ripped curtains and hangings aside, and swore at frightened servants. It was not in search of any London criminal that they had come, Francis knew that. They needed an excuse to ransack the house, and this was as good as any. Silently he prayed that Cuthbert had managed to get away.

Now the raiders, Grenville at their head, had clattered upstairs and were banging at the door of the steward's room, cursing because it was locked.

"May I open it for you gentlemen?" asked a calm voice behind them. Turning, the sheriff and his men found themselves looking into Cuthbert's gray, unafraid eyes.

"Who are you, fellow?" the sheriff demanded, seizing him roughly by the front of his jerkin.

"I am a man," replied Cuthbert simply.

"Do you jest with me, sirrah!" yelled Grenville. He seemed about to strike Cuthbert, but he checked himself as his fingers closed upon something round underneath the simple garment.

Ripping open the jerkin he pulled out a small, circular leather case, hung by a cord round his victim's neck. Inside it was a wax disc, stamped with an unmistakable picture. The Lamb of God.

Eyes ablaze with triumph and hatred, Grenville tore the Agnus Dei from its cord and brandished it before his men.

"A man, are you?" he yelled, turning back to Cuthbert. "A priest, more likely!"

By the time Cuthbert Mayne left the house as a

prisoner, the persecutors had found something even more damaging. Among the books and papers in the room was a Latin document, unmistakably a papal bull, or at least a copy of one. Was this not the notorious document which had excommunicated the English queen and absolved her Catholic subjects from their allegiance to her?

No, it was not. It was simply a copy of the bull issued during the recent Jubilee Year and contained nothing that could possibly make Cuthbert a traitor. His persecutors, not the men to let such a detail stand in their way, used it just the same when they framed their charges against him.

More than 40 years have passed since John Houghton and his companions were butchered at Tyburn. England is now a Protestant country ruled by the first Elizabeth, daughter of Henry and Anne Boleyn. Not herself an ardent Protestant, she is a coolly pragmatic ruler who, during these early years of her reign, thinks it best to let the Catholic religion die a natural death.

Sooner or later, Elizabeth reasoned, the priests ordained during the preceding reign of Mary, her Catholic half sister, must grow old and die. Were no new priests to replace them there would be no Mass and no Catholicism.

New priests there were, however. Already at work secretly up and down the land, young Englishmen trained abroad in seminaries established for the purpose. These were men prepared to face every kind of danger and discomfort to keep the faith alive, men prepared, if necessary, to die. Of the hundreds of "seminary priests" who were to make that sacrifice, Cuthbert Mayne was the first.

Like many of the martyrs who were to follow him,

Cuthbert was a convert to the Catholic faith. A Devon man, born at Youlston, near Barnstaple, he was brought up by a priest-uncle who had succumbed to the state religion. Hardly had he left grammar school when, at the age of 18 or 19, he found himself an ordained Anglican minister, though he had no particular inclination towards the life and certainly no great preparation. His uncle had decided where young Cuthbert's future lay.

Sent to Oxford, he became chaplain to St. John's College and made friends with two men of outstanding scholarship, Gregory Martin and Edmund Campion. At this time Edmund, the future Jesuit, was himself still a deacon in Anglican orders.

When Edmund became unhappy about his spiritual state he must surely have confided in Cuthbert. When his brilliant friend left the university and, after a spell in Ireland, wrote from France to say that he was studying for the Catholic priesthood, the news must have shaken Cuthbert as it shook many others who had known Edmund at Oxford. Gregory Martin was already in the same seminary, at Douai, and in letter after letter his two friends begged Cuthbert to abandon the Church of England and follow them abroad.

By this time Cuthbert himself was profoundly disturbed, for other Catholic friends had joined with Edmund and Gregory in persuading him that he was wrong to remain an Anglican. Yet he loved the peace of his Oxford college and the company which he found there, and he could not bear to think of leaving it all behind for a future which promised poverty and danger. His mild and gentle nature made him popular with everyone, Catholic and Protestant alike. In Oxford, surely, he could be happy until the end of his days.

Yet he was not happy, for his conscience continued to torment him. For several years he tried to ignore it as he clung to his secure and well-paid career.

In the end, his hand was forced. In 1570, soon after Cuthbert had taken an M.A. degree, one of the letters from Douai fell into the hands of the Protestant Bishop of London. He immediately sent a pursuivant—a hunter of papists—to Oxford to arrest everyone named in the letter.

Cuthbert was out of town at the time, but he might have returned to Oxford and walked into the trap had not a friend named John Ford, himself later.to be martyred, warned him that he was a wanted man.

To Cuthbert it was clear that God had taken a hand. He could dither no longer. Though he abjured Protestantism soon after his narrow escape, it was not until 1573 that he arrived at Douai. Why he delayed we do not know. Perhaps, like his friend Edmund, he needed time to discover his vocation to the priesthood; perhaps he simply had to wait nearly three years for an opportunity to slip out of the country.

In April, 1576, he was back, a priest now, eager to make up for his years as an Anglican by risking his life for the true Church. With him came John Payne, a Northamptonshire man who had also been ordained at Douai.

Having passed safely through the port inspection, the two priests separated. John made for Essex, the county lying to the east of London, while Cuthbert headed west to Cornwall.

Provided by Francis Tregian with a home and a cover job, he travelled the county for more than a year, saying Mass and hearing confessions in barns, cellars, the upper rooms of great houses, always one jump ahead of Elizabeth's priest hunters. It was a strange life in an England where, well within living memory,

Mass had been freely celebrated in every town and village. Yet in years to come generations of priests were to spend their entire ministry on the run.

Who alerted the authorities to Cuthbert's whereabouts we do not know. Perhaps there was a Judas in his congregation; perhaps some sharp-eyed Protestant spotted Mr. Tregian's steward in circumstances which made him suspect Cuthbert's real function. What is certain is that when Grenville and his gang descended on the house at Golden, they knew whom they would find there.

Taunted by their captors, Cuthbert and his employer were taken the 40 miles to Launceston, with several stops at Protestant houses along the way. Though he made no attempt to escape, during these rest intervals Cuthbert was marched upstairs and tied to bedposts, a humiliation which he bore with his customary cheerfulness.

At Launceston he was kept in a filthy cell until the next Michaelmas assizes, when he was tried and condemned on trumped-up charges which were to become all too familiar in the future.

One of the judges, Manwood, directed the jury to find Cuthbert guilty, and they did so. Because the second judge, Jeffrey, had qualms about the proceedings, the conviction was reviewed by the whole judicial bench, sitting in London. Their opinion was divided, with the majority on Cuthbert's side. The case went up to the Privy Council, who ruled that the conviction should stand as a warning to other priests coming from beyond the seas.

The excommunication of Elizabeth had inevitably sharpened opposition to the missionaries, for now every Catholic was regarded as a potential traitor. They were not aided, either, by exiled fellow countrymen who plotted the queen's overthrow by foreign troops in the mistaken belief that Catholics at home would welcome this "liberation." Among the schemers was the rector of Douai himself, Dr. William Allen, who was later to become a cardinal.

On the day before his execution, Cuthbert was offered his life if he would swear to the queen's ecclesiastical supremacy. Asking for a Bible, he kissed it and declared, "The queen neither ever was, nor is, nor ever shall be head of the Church of England."

When he was tied to the hurdle, some cruel magistrates urged the deputy sheriff to let his head hang over the back so that it would be battered along the cobblestones as the horses dragged him the quarter mile to the market place. Though Cuthbert actually offered to undergo this added suffering, the deputy sheriff refused to inflict it.

On the scaffold one of the magistrates tried to make him implicate Francis Tregian and another Catholic gentleman. He refused. Then, as Cuthbert commended his soul to God, the hangman turned him off the ladder.

His enemies yelled at the hangman to cut him down while he was still conscious, so that he might feel the full torment of the disembowelling. Once again the deputy sheriff would have none of their cruelty and Cuthbert remained unconscious under the knife to the end.

Cuthbert Mayne died on November 30, 1577, a secular priest like so many of those who were to follow him. Edmund Campion, his friend of Oxford days, had gone to Douai with no thought of entering a Religious Order or, so far as we know, of returning to England as a missionary. Many English and Welsh priests chose, for one reason or another, to live out their lives in exile and Edmund might very easily have remained at

Douai, as Gregory Martin did, teaching and helping to translate the great Douai Bible.

He had spent two years at the French seminary when he decided that it was in the still new Society of Jesus that his vocation lay. How Edmund came to this conclusion not even Jesuit historians have been able to show precisely, for it is unlikely that at this time he had ever met a Jesuit or heard one preach. Most certainly, however, he knew their reputation and he had possibly read the Spiritual Exercises of St. Ignatius.

It must have been with some surprise, not to mention pleasure, that the father general greeted the weary young Englishman who had walked the hundreds of miles to Rome to offer himself as a recruit. It was not every day that a candidate of Edmund's talents appeared on his doorstep.

The son of a London bookseller, Edmund Campion entered Oxford at 15 and by 17 was a fellow of St. John's College and the university's foremost Latin orator. Admirers crowded into his lectures, aping his mannerisms, his clothes, and his tricks of speech—even calling themselves "Campionists." Queen Elizabeth, visiting Oxford, was deeply impressed by young Master Campion's debating skills. In the Church of England, few doubted, Edmund would reach the very top.

Few suspected that the brilliant young deacon was deeply troubled about his Anglicanism. More and more his studies of Scripture and the Fathers of the Church convinced him that Christ's authority belonged to the Catholic Church alone.

Already some of his friends had left Oxford for Douai and were urging him to follow them, just as he was later to urge the wavering Cuthbert Mayne. At the same time, as Catholicism began to gain ground in

England, Edmund was asked to defend the state
Church in an open-air sermon before the London
public.

Torn in conscience, he escaped for a while to
Ireland, where he wrote a history of the country and
attempted, unsuccessfully, to found a university. If the
tide turned in the Church's favor, he told himself, he
might yet find an honorable career as a Catholic
layman. The Pope's excommunication of Elizabeth
laid to rest that hope.

Edmund seems to have made up his mind to leave
for Douai after attending, in disguise, the trial of John
Storey, an elderly priest against whom Elizabeth and
her ministers had a grudge. Kidnapped in Antwerp, he
was brought back to London and executed with particular cruelty.

Now that he was a Jesuit he must have prepared
himself never to see his homeland again. Though
several other Englishmen already belonged to the
Society of Jesus, there was no English province and no
Jesuit mission to England. When news spread that a
famous Oxford scholar had joined the ranks, a regular
battle of the provincials began, each one eager to
secure the prize.

It was to the Austrian province that Edmund was
eventually sent. At Brno, in what is now Czechoslova-
kia, he spent a happy novitiate sweeping corridors and
working on the farm—tasks which he seems to have
enjoyed even more than the theological studies which
followed at Prague. Ordained in 1578, he was appointed to the Prague college staff. It looked as though
he was to live the academic life after all.

Only a year later, however, Dr. Allen, his old rector
at Douai, asked that some Jesuits be sent to assist his
own priests on the English mission. One of the first to
be chosen was Edmund Campion.

Before dawn on June 25, 1580, a certain Mr. Edmunds, a jewel merchant by trade, stepped ashore at Dover from a ship in which he and his manservant had sailed from the French port of St. Omer. Secret agents had warned the government to expect Jesuits, and a special watch had been set at the ports. Mr. Edmunds and his servant aroused suspicion at once.

The mayor of Dover himself presided over their interrogation, but could find nothing wrong with their story. After a period abroad the merchant was returning to London to sell his wares in a market which had become highly favorable. Within a few hours the suspects were released.

"Mr. Edmunds" was, of course, none other than Edmund Campion. His companion was a Jesuit lay brother, Ralph Emerson.

When he reached London Edmund found that, far from welcoming the Jesuit missionaries, many Catholics feared that they would only bring more persecution down on Catholic heads. The biggest fear was that the Jesuits might plot to overthrow the queen, as Allen and his friends were doing from the safety of France and Italy. The scheming exiles had seriously misread the mood at home; despite government measures against them, the vast majority of English Catholics remained loyal to their Protestant sovereign and wanted no foreign intervention.

To allay their fears Edmund and his Jesuit colleagues swore an oath that they had come to England purely for the good of souls and that they would undertake no political action of any kind. What swiftly won over the Catholics, however, was the skill and dedication which they brought to their dangerous ministry. Persecution had brought with it new and difficult cases of conscience with which Jesuits were especially trained to deal. Soon Catholics who had dreaded their coming were eagerly seeking them as confessors.

As he moved around the country, constantly changing his name and disguise, Edmund frequently read, or was told by people who knew for an absolute fact, that Campion, the notorious Jesuit, was taken. He wrote to the father general in Rome of the "exceeding reverence" in which the Jesuits were held, and begged him to send more men, the best he could provide, to the English mission, where "the harvest is exceeding great."

He had many narrow escapes. During one raid he would certainly have been taken had not a maid, with great presence of mind, pushed him into a pond and told the pursuers angrily that he was a too forward admirer. Edmund, covered in mud, was unrecognized.

Knowing that he must ultimately be caught, and that he would then have little chance to explain why the Jesuits had come to England, he published the remarkable document known as "Campion's Brag," a message to the English people in which he stressed the nonpolitical nature of the Jesuits' work and begged for an opportunity to debate the Catholic case with leading Anglican theologians. Queen Elizabeth herself, he suggested, might care to be present during these discussions! The final, moving passage of Edmund's address has often been quoted:

> Many innocent hands are lifted up to heaven for you daily by those English students, whose posteritie shall never die, which beyond seas, gathering virtue and sufficient knowledge for the purpose, are determined never to give you over, but either to win you to heaven, or to die upon your pikes. And touching our Societie, be it known to you that we have made a league—all the Jesuits in the world, whose succession and multitude must overreach all the practices of

England—cheerfully to carry the cross you shall lay upon us, and never to despair your recovery, while we have a man left to enjoy your Tyburn, or to be racked with your torments, or consumed with your prisons. The expense is reckoned, the enterprise is begun; it is of God, it cannot be withstood. So the faith was planted: so it must be restored. . . ."

Edmund followed up the "Brag" with an address in Latin to the learned world, the *Decem Rationes*. Printed secretly and in conditions of the greatest difficulty, this caused a new sensation when it appeared overnight on the benches of the University Church in Oxford. It set out ten reasons why Edmund was convinced that he could successfully defend Catholic claims against the Anglicans.

The *Decem Rationes* was written chiefly while Edmund was preaching in Lancashire, a strongly Catholic county, where his sermons were remembered 50 years afterwards by those who heard them. All the time spies pursued him and several times he was nearly caught.

The success of his latest work enraged the authorities and made him England's most wanted man. As the priest hunters redoubled their efforts, Edmund headed for Norfolk, where his enemies would not expect to find him.

During the journey south he said Mass at Lyford Grange, home of the Yate family. He had already departed when the Catholic neighbors heard that the great Father Campion had been at the Grange. Tracked down to an inn near Oxford, Edward was prevailed upon to turn back and say Mass there once more before going on his way.

In the congregation this time was George Eliot, formerly manservant to several Catholic families, who had lately been arrested on charges of rape and homicide and who had obtained his release by promising to work as a priest catcher. Immediately after Mass Eliot slipped out, returning at 1:00 P.M. with a search squad.

For hours the searchers ransacked the Grange, but no trace of Edmund could they find. Only on the following morning, when they were almost ready to give up, did they find Edmund and Fathers Ford and Collington, two other priests who had been staying there, hiding together in a secret chamber near the top of the house.

When the captors left for London with their prey, they had a fourth prisoner. Father William Filby, knowing nothing of the raid, had called at the Grange and walked into their arms.

As the procession neared the capital, the prisoners were pinioned. To Edmund was fixed a label: "This is Campion, the seditious Jesuit." No doubt this humiliation, ordered by the government, hurt his guards more that it hurt Edmund, for by this time they had all been completely won over by his kindness and charm. Even Eliot, whose conscience now appeared to trouble him, was assured of his victim's forgiveness.

"If thou repent and come to confession, I will absolve thee," Edmund told him. "But large penance must thou have."

In the Tower Edmund was held for four days in the notorious "Little Ease," a cramped torture cell where he could neither stand nor lie down. After four days, much to his surprise, he was taken from the cell, put into a boat and rowed up river to meet Queen Elizabeth face to face.

The sovereign and her aides tried to persuade Edmund to abandon his Catholic faith and return to Anglicanism, where a prosperous future would be his. Courteously but firmly Edmund refused.

Back in the Tower he was racked three times in an

effort to make him betray Catholic friends. He had promised that "come rack, come rope," he would never talk, and he kept his word. Asked afterwards how he felt, he replied, "Not ill, because not at all."

Only after this ill treatment was he granted his longed for confrontation with Anglican theologians. Denied books or writing materials, he routed them completely. In vain he dared them to show him their copies of St. Augustine and St. John Chrysostom so that he could point out the quotations which he hurled at them from memory. They could only respond by jeering when he made a slip of the tongue in Greek.

At his trial Edmund defended himself with equal vigor. Though the verdict was a foregone conclusion, it took a packed jury a whole hour to find Edmund and his codefendants guilty.

One of those sentenced with him was Ralph Sherwin, like Edmund a former Oxford don who had been reconciled to the Church while teaching at the university. Ordained at Douai, he had gone on to the English College in Rome, where he was involved in the quarrels between English and Welsh students which caused the college to be put under Jesuit direction.

The Rome students were required to swear that, once ordained, they would offer themselves for the English mission. When he took his oath Ralph added these words: *Potius hodie quam cras* (Rather today than tomorrow).

Edmund and Ralph travelled across Europe in a party which included both Jesuits and student priests, and whose members later split up and came to England separately. In Geneva they had much fun disputing with Protestant ministers in the street until midnight. Gleefully, Ralph wrote a friend in Rome,

"We met one of the Calvinist ministers and buckled with him in questions about their Church until we almost made the fellow mad."

Arrested in London after three months of successful preaching, he was taken to the Marshalsea prison, where his high spirits did not desert him. Heavily chained, he wrote a priest who was still at large, "I wear now on my feet and legs some little bells to keep me in mind who I am and whose I am. I never heard such sweet harmony before."

Like Edmund he refused to apostatize, even though he was offered a bishopric if he would do so. Like Edmund he was racked—and was left to lie out all night in the snow before being brought in and tortured again.

Afterwards he lay for five days without food and drink, "as he thought in a sleep, before our Savior on the cross." When he regained consciousness, he felt no pain in his limbs.

In Westminster Hall young Ralph Sherwin, too, looked at his judges with a firm eye. "The plain reason of our standing here," he declared, "is religion, not treason."

He regarded the death sentence as a victory and wrote from the Tower to his uncle: "Innocency is my only comfort against all the forged villainy which is fathered on my fellow priests and me. . . . God forgive all injustice, and if it be his blessed will to convert our persecutors, that they may become professors of his truth . . . And so, my good old John, farewell."

Two days before the end he met Edmund Campion in the Tower grounds. "Ah, Father Campion," he said. "I shall soon be above yonder fellow."

They were dragged to Tyburn with a third priest, Alexander Briant. He, too, had been reconciled to the Church at Oxford and had been ordained at Douai. As the hurdles drew near to their destination the watching crowd craned forward for a sight of the condemned men. What they saw astonished them. "But they laugh, they do not care for death!" they cried.

Edmund, the first to die, was rebuked for praying in Latin rather than in English. He replied mildly that he would "pray God in a language that they both well understood." His last words were a prayer for the queen.

Next the hangman seized Ralph. "Come Sherwin," he snarled, "take thou also thy wages." Ralph kissed the hands, covered with Edmund's blood, and climbed into the cart.

By now the spectators were full of sympathy for the victims. "Good Mr. Sherwin, the Lord God receive your soul," they cried out, and continued to say it for some time after he was dead.

Ralph Sherwin lived and died a secular priest. Alexander Briant, though a secular priest throughout his short ministry, wrote from prison to ask for admission to the Society of Jesus. He was accepted in his absence and is now numbered among the Jesuit martyrs.

We have the word of the torturer himself, one Norton, that Alexander was racked more severely than any of his other victims. So great was the public disgust when his cruelty became known that Norton himself was jailed for a few days to save the government's face.

When his tormentor threatened to stretch him a foot longer than God had made him, Alexander answered him defiantly and set his mind firmly on the sufferings of our Lord. As a result, he told the Jesuits in his letter, he seemed to feel no pain. "Whether this that I say be miraculous or no, God He knoweth," he added, "but true it is." It was during the torture that he resolved to enter the Society.

He fashioned a little cross of wood for himself and looked at it continually during the trial. When it was eventually snatched from him he retorted, "You may tear it from my hands, but you cannot take it from my heart. Nay, I shall die for Him who first died on it for me."

Die he did, at the age of 28. Despite all his sufferings his face remained serene, almost angelic. Once again the Tyburn crowd was deeply moved.

Edmund Campion, Ralph Sherwin, and Alexander Briant died on December 1, 1581. Though he was condemned with them, it was not until May 30 of the following year that Luke Kirby took the road to Tyburn.

Born in Yorkshire, Luke probably graduated from Cambridge before studying for the priesthood at Douai and at the English College in Rome. Though Yorkshiremen are sometimes said to be tight-fisted, Luke plainly was not, for he once plucked the shirt from his back and presented it to a Roman beggar.

He crossed Europe with Edmund Campion's party, but was captured as soon as he arrived at Dover and in the Tower was tortured with the "scavenger's daughter," a broad hoop of iron, fastened by a hinge, which was passed under the legs of the kneeling prisoner and then fastened over the small of his back, so that his body was compressed. Though he was left in this state for more than an hour, the torturers got nothing out of him.

Soon afterwards Luke and other priests were forced to listen to a Calvinist sermon filled with anti-Catholic abuse. They gave the preacher a hard time, constantly interrupting him with their counterarguments. During his imprisonment friends smuggled a Mass kit into

Luke's cell, and the corporal which he used is pre-served, with other relics, at Stoneyhurst College in Lancashire.

One more canonized martyr belongs to this chapter, one whom we have met briefly already. John Payne, who crossed to England with Cuthbert Mayne, minis-tered in Essex for more than five years before he was eventually betrayed by the same George Eliot who brought Edmund Campion to his death.

Like Cuthbert, John ostensibly worked as a steward in a Catholic household while secretly travelling the county on his priestly mission. Three months after his arrival, he wrote, just as Edmund Campion had done, to ask for more priests. "In increasing numbers a great many are reconciled to the Catholic Church," he reported. "The heretics are greatly troubled by the very name of Douai priests, which fills all Catholics with consolation."

The treacherous Eliot had obtained a post as servant to John's employer, Lady Anne Petre, at Ingatestone. John was arrested after Eliot had handed to the gov-ernment a list of priests and their probable where-abouts. John, he alleged, had tried to persuade him to kill the queen.

Twice racked in an effort to make him confess, John constantly maintained his innocence. Crippled by torture he dictated, "I pray God long to preserve Her Highness, unto whom I have always wished no worse than to my own soul. I forgive Eliot his monstrous wickedness."

Condemned for treason on the unsupported evi-dence of Eliot, John also forgave the jury as "poor simple men, nothing at all understanding what treason is."

Though he remained gentle and patient towards everyone, he confided to a Catholic friend that the

Protestant ministers who tried to make him apostatize "by their foolish babbling did much vex and trouble him."

For his execution, on April 2, 1582, John Payne was taken from the Tower to Chelmsford, the county town of Essex. Here he kissed the gallows, forgave all who had harmed him, including Eliot by name, and asked forgiveness of any whom he had offended.

"All the town loved him exceedingly," reported an eyewitness, "and so did the keepers. No man seemed to mislike him, but much sorrowed and lamented his death."

The good folk of Chelmsford could not save him but they could, and did, make sure that he suffered at the end as little as possible. "They very courteously caused men to hang on his feet, and set the knot to his ear, commanding Bull, the hangman from Newgate, to despatch in the quartering of him lest, as they said, he should revive."

Their action must surely have been reported to Elizabeth and her ministers, along with the display of sympathy shown to the martyrs at Tyburn. It had no effect; the killing went on—and the Church grew stronger as the martyrs shed their blood.

3

A Jesting Fellow

It was not every day that a schoolmaster sat in the stocks, and the crowd gathered round to make the most of the spectacle.

The victim, hands and feet securely fastened, grinned back at them as though he were actually enjoying his situation. A vagabond, a chicken thief, or a scolding wife would now be trying vainly to duck away from a shower of rotten vegetables and other missiles. But something about Richard Gwyn made even the town urchins stay their hands.

A large, red-nosed man, a minister of the Protestant church, stepped forward frowning. The fellow must not be allowed to escape unscathed; he must be shown the error of his ways.

"You papists," he began importantly, "claim that St. Peter has the power of the keys. Well, I have to tell you, as a parson of the established Church, that I, no less than the apostle, have that same power."

Through dancing eyes the schoolmaster regarded him for a moment. With a grin broader than ever he nodded towards his opponent's proboscis.

"My friend, it was the keys of the kingdom of heaven that St. Peter received," he retorted. "You have received the keys of the beer cellar!"

The crowd roared its delight as the clerical toper stepped back, spluttering with indignation.

Nobody could put Richard Gwyn down. Arrested for nonattendance at Protestant services, he had been carried by force, his hands and feet chained, to the church at Ruthin. There he interrupted so loudly, and rattled his chains so vigorously, that the sermon could hardly be heard.

So here he was in the stocks, forced to listen to the ministers who came by the hour to harangue him. Needless to say, none of them made the slightest impact.

Richard Gwyn had himself been brought up a Protestant. Born at Llanidloes, in the very heart of Wales, he went as a teenager to Oxford but transferred to Cambridge, where he took his degree.

In 1537, the year of Richard's birth, Henry VIII had already cut the tie with Rome and was laying his greedy hands on the monasteries. Yet the Wales to which the young graduate returned was still strongly Catholic and remained so for many years to come. Many of the great families and most of the common people remained loyal to the old faith.

Richard's own doubts may well have begun while he was still at the university. Yet he did not, like so many of his contemporaries, become a Catholic and go abroad to study for the priesthood. Instead, remaining outwardly a Protestant, he opened a school in the Flintshire village of Overton. He also married and became the father of a family which, by the time of his arrest, numbered six children.

His nonattendance at the Anglican church was soon noticed and words were whispered in his ear. He should, he was reminded, set an example to his pupils. It would not look well if the village schoolmaster were to be suspected of popery.

So Richard dragged his reluctant feet to Divine Service, despising himself as he went. How many of those around him, he wondered as he sat uneasily in his pew, were in church because they dared not stay away? He knew that many, like himself, had families to support, families who would suffer if the head of the house were heavily fined or jailed.

"The peace of God, which passeth all understanding, keep your hearts and minds in the knowledge and love of God, and of his Son, Jesus Christ our Lord . . . ."

With the blessing came release, and Richard walked slowly from the little church. Though his own language was Welsh, he could appreciate well enough the fine, rolling English of the Book of Common Prayer. Yet for all its dignified clothing, the service which he had attended was no substitute for the Mass, which Welshmen had offered unchallenged in their hills and valleys for more than a thousand years.

During the weeks that followed, Richard's normally cheerful face often wore a strained, worried expression. His pupils wondered why their kindly teacher often seemed scarcely to hear when they asked him a question, and why he had so few jokes, now, to lighten the tedium of Latin grammar.

He must become a Catholic, Richard knew that. Indeed, he had known it for a long time. Yet if he did take the final step he would have to give up the school into which he had put so much of his life. And what would become then of his wife and little children?

A meeting with a seminary priest put an end to Richard's agonizing. As he listened to the young man, himself risking his life to bring the Mass to North

Wales, Richard Gwyn knew that he could delay his conversion no longer.

Now that he was a Catholic Richard himself was forced to lead an existence that was partly underground, for papist schoolmasters, especially, were marked men. In 1580, when the government ordered a crackdown on the Catholic community, the order made special mention of "all schoolmasters, public or private."

By that time Richard had already had one narrow escape, when a Protestant cleric, himself an apostate, recognized him on the streets of Wrexham and denounced him. Though actually arrested, he managed to free himself and resume his teaching. For some time his school was an old barn where he taught his pupils their conjugations and declensions and urged them always to remain loyal to *yr hen Fam,* the old Mother Church.

A fresh arrest was, of course, only a matter of time. Richard must have known that he could not long remain undiscovered. A schoolmaster was, after all, a sitting target. He could not, as the priests did, keep on the move and constantly change his name and his disguise.

It was in July, 1580, only a month after the government edict, that Richard Gwyn once more found himself in prison. From his cell at Ruthin he was brought before a judge who offered him his freedom if he would conform. When he refused he was sent back to jail, where he remained until the following May.

It was after this second appearance before an assize judge that he was taken forcibly to church—not, it seems, without a struggle on Richard's part, for it took six sheriff's men to carry him, heels upwards, to his place beneath the pulpit. One cannot help but pity the unfortunate preacher, one Thomas Jones.

For brawling in church and for refusing to attend

Anglican services, Richard was fined the equivalent of about $10,000.

"What means have you got to meet the fine?" asked the judge severely.

"I have got something towards it," Richard answered with a smile.

"How much?"

"Sixpence," replied Richard brightly—and went straight back to prison with the irons on his legs doubled. Altogether he remained in prison for four years and was tortured three times, but would tell his persecutors nothing.

In October, 1584, at Wrexham, he made his eighth appearance in the assize court dock. This time the charge was treason, and Richard must have realized what was coming. It was alleged that he had tried to reconcile a man named Gronow to the Church of Rome and had also maintained the supremacy of the Pope. Richard denied that he had ever spoken to Gronow. What local people thought of the trial we may judge from the attitude of the jury, who failed to appear.

A new jury was empanelled on the spot. They asked the judge whom they were to convict and whom to acquit!

Of the two men charged with Richard one was, in fact, acquitted. His name was Morris and he had given way under torture. When the verdict was announced the poor fellow wept bitterly. Overcome with remorse, he wanted to die a martyr with his friends.

At this point Richard's wife was brought into court, her youngest child in her arms, and warned not to imitate her husband.

"If you lack blood," she replied proudly, "you may take my life as well as my husband's. If you will give the witnesses a little bribe they will give evidence against me, too!"

Though sentenced to death with Richard, the third defendant, John Hughes, was afterwards reprieved. On October 17, 1584, Richard Gwyn was dragged to his death alone.

As he left the prison he found a crowd waiting to bid him farewell. Many were his former pupils and some were in tears.

"Weep not for me," he told them, "for I do but pay the rent before the rent day."

His wife, the little one again in her arms, knelt to receive his blessing. It was raining heavily.

At the scaffold the hangman, Cotynor, also knelt to ask his victim's forgiveness. "I do forgive thee before God," replied Richard, "and I wish thee no more harm than I wish my own heart."

As he climbed the ladder, he said to the crowd, "I have been a jesting fellow, and if I have offended any that way, or by my poems, I beseech them for God's sake to forgive me."

The crowd called out that he should be allowed to die before the disembowelling began. The sheriff, another apostate, refused. Richard suffered the full agony of the sentence.

During his years in jail Richard composed a number of poems, some of them, indeed, bitterly anti-Protestant in tone. At the end of one, however, comes this verse:

> *O daw gofyn pwy ai cant,*
> *Athro plant o Cymro*
> *Sydd yn cymryd carchar beth,*
> *Yn buw mewn gobeth etto.*

> If there comes a question who sang it,
> A Welsh teacher of children,
> Who is undergoing imprisonment,
> Yet lives in hope.

4
Heroines

Hearing a woman's footsteps hurrying along the narrow streets of York, neighbors looked out and observed the slim figure of Margaret Clitherow hurrying through the twilight towards the house of her friends the Vavasours. If Margaret was going out at this hour, there must be another baby on the way.

As an adjunct to his medical practice, Dr. Vavasour ran a sort of maternity home where Margaret frequently acted as midwife. At least, the neighbors believed that she did. As they watched her go, they must have shaken their heads admiringly. A skilled butcher who ran her husband's shop, a clear-headed businesswoman, mother of a young family—and a midwife, too! Quite a remarkable young woman, young Mrs. Clitherow.

Energetic and versatile though she certainly was, Margaret was no midwife. The Vavasours were Catholic and she was on her way there for instruction from a priest whom they were hiding. For Margaret Clitherow had herself decided to join the Church of Rome.

What her husband, easygoing John, thought of her decision we do not know for sure, but it appears that he was not seriously disturbed. John was a Protestant and remained one to the end of his days—not, almost certainly, from any profound conviction, but because those who belonged to the state Church could more easily stay out of trouble and mind their takings. If his wife wanted to recite rosaries and pray for the dead, well, that was all right, so long as she did not advertise her religion or let it interfere with business.

From what we know of John's personality, and we know a good deal, he probably reasoned this way. If so he was sadly misjudging his wife; he, more than anyone, should have realized that it was not in her nature to lie low and pretend. When Margaret Clitherow gave herself, she gave totally.

Like her husband, Margaret had been brought up a Protestant. Her father was Thomas Middleton, a prosperous York wax chandler. He died when she was only 11 and it was her stepfather, an ambitious innkeeper named Henry May, who arranged young Margaret Middleton's marriage to the widowed John Clitherow. At the age of 15 Margaret found herself with two stepchildren to raise, a home and a staff of servants to run, and the shop in the Shambles to manage.

The Shambles is still there today and so is the shop, though it is now a shrine where Mass is offered. The whole street is, indeed, much more sedate than it must have been in Margaret's day, when it consisted entirely of butchers' shops and rang to the sound of axes, of men in bloodied aprons crying their wares, and of housewives gossiping and haggling.

Nobody watching Margaret at work would have guessed that she hated the butchery trade. Calmly and efficiently she supervised the assistants, attended to customers, and cast up the accounts. Yet often she begged John to give up the shop and concentrate on the wholesale side of the business.

In the home, which lay behind the shop, Margaret was equally a perfectionist. She had a sharp tongue, and servants who were slipshod soon learned to fear it. Yet she would herself, once she became a Catholic, willingly perform the most humble tasks. "God forbid," she would say, "that I should will any to do that in my house which I would not willingly do myself first."

Margaret had been married for three years when she was converted and had by then borne John a son, little Henry. Almost certainly she had been in the crowd which saw Thomas Percy, earl of Northumberland, beheaded at York for his part in the Northern Rising which attempted to free Mary, Queen of Scots, and to secure toleration for Catholics. "If I had a thousand lives, I would give them up for the Catholic faith," he declared as he laid his head on the block. The words must have made a deep impression on her.

Whether it was the earl's death which prompted her decision we do not know, but certainly she was received into the Church shortly after it. She joined a flourishing underground community of Catholics and was soon busy spreading the faith among her friends.

It was in August, 1577, that Margaret received her first jail sentence, after previously paying fines for refusing to attend the Anglican Church. By now she had a daughter, Anne, and a second son, whose name we do not know, had probably also been born.

Despite the anguish which separation from the youngsters must have cost her, Margaret described prison as "a most happy and profitable school." Here, priests and layfolk lived a quasimonastic life, praying and studying together, appointing a superior and following their own Rule. Since warders were easily bribed, priests from the city often came in to say Mass.

In prison the forceful young woman gained a new maturity, learned to rely on God rather than on herself, and strove to curb her tongue. In prison, too, she learned to read and write, and to understand simple Latin.

After her first release in June, 1578, she set up a secret Mass center in the house next to her own, with access from the Clitherow premises. Her husband must have been well aware of its existence, but kept the secret. When Mass was over Margaret served breakfast to everyone, even those in the humblest walk of life.

Twice more Margaret was jailed and twice more released. During her third prison term, in 1583, her confessor, Father William Hart, was executed in York. The very next year, Margaret sent young Henry abroad to study for the priesthood.

The Throckmorton plot, a futile attempt to put Mary, Queen of Scots, on the English throne, brought a fresh wave of government action against Catholics. All Jesuits and seminary priests were ordered to leave England within 40 days, and students for the priesthood were ordered to return.

To Henry May, now lord mayor of York, a stepdaughter like Margaret must have been an acute embarrassment. There is a strong suspicion that when Margaret's home was again raided, on March 10, 1586, Henry May was behind the move, though surely he could not have foreseen what terrible consequences would follow.

When they burst into the house the sheriff's men found Margaret going about her tasks normally. The priest, in his hiding place upstairs, heard the commotion below and made a swift escape. In a ground floor room a class of children, some Margaret's, some belonging to friends, were having a school lesson from a Catholic scholar whom Margaret had hired as a teacher.

Seizing one of the pupils, a little Flemish boy, the armed ruffians threatened him with a beating if he did not tell them where the priest was hidden. Though they did not catch the priest they got from the terrified child a list of all those whom he had seen at Mass in the secret chapel. Everyone in the house, the youngsters included, was hauled off to jail, where Margaret's children were severely whipped for their faith.

Told that she would be prosecuted for harboring a priest—a capital offense—Margaret laughed. "I wish I had something to give you for this good news," she replied. "Wait, take this fig—I have nothing better."

Margaret continued to laugh and joke until she stepped into the dock. There she astonished everyone by refusing to enter a plea.

Nobody was more taken aback than the presiding judge, a humane man named Clench who clearly did not want to see her die. In vain he pointed out that the prosecution had a weak case and that she might well be acquitted. Margaret would not budge.

Coaxing, threats, shock tactics—all failed to move her. In an effort to make her plead not guilty, the judges even had two ruffians dressed in Mass vestments fool about with unconsecrated hosts. The buffoonery did not break her down.

Exasperated, Clench warned her that a terrible death awaited defendants who refused to enter a plea. Margaret replied that she would be happy to die for so holy a cause.

Though he and his colleagues must have thought her mad, Margaret had good reasons for her stubbornness. Convinced that the jury had been ordered to find her guilty, she would not allow her death to rest on their consciences. If there were a trial her children would be brought to give evidence against her, and this she would not tolerate. Nor would she risk the betrayal of Catholic friends which a trial would involve.

Sent back to jail for the night to consider her position, Margaret reappeared in the dock to face more coaxing from the worried judge. "We see no reason why you should refuse," he urged. "Here be but small witness against you."

"Indeed," replied Margaret dryly, "I think you have no witnesses against me but children, whom with an apple and a rod you make to say what you will."

Clench hinted that even if the verdict went against her, she might still be shown mercy. Margaret remained obdurate.

At his side Clench had a brother judge who was determined to make an example of this too clever butcher's wife. Impatiently, he urged his colleague to cease paltering and to pronounce the sentence decreed by law for those who stood "mute of malice."

Reluctantly Clench spoke the terrible words. Margaret must be stripped naked, laid on the ground, and left for three days with as much weight upon her as she was able to bear. During this time she would be fed only a little barley bread and puddle water. On the third day she would be pressed to death, her hands and feet tied to posts and a sharp stone under her back.

"I would to God my husband and children might suffer with me for so good a cause," Margaret replied calmly.

When he heard the news, John Clitherow wept so violently that the blood gushed from his nose. "Let them take all I have and save her," he sobbed. "She is the best wife in England and the best Catholic also."

Since there was a possibility that Margaret might be pregnant, Clench ordered a ten-day stay of execution. This did not please officials, who, as Margaret had correctly judged, were determined to make an example of her.

As the day of her death drew near Margaret fasted and prayed constantly for the grace to remain steadfast to the end. Told that she would die on March 25, the day on which her stay of execution expired, Margaret once more gave thanks to God.

She spent the last night in the company of a kindly Protestant woman, Mrs. Yoward, who had been thrown into prison for debt. For a time the two women prayed together, then Margaret prayed alone for many hours. Finally, she stretched out beside the hearth and slept to prepare herself for the ordeal to come.

When the sheriff's men came for her they found her dressed like a bride, with ribbons in her hair. Barefoot she walked from the Ouse Bridge prison to a building known as the Tolbooth, smiling and handing out money to the crowd.

Before she set out she had sent her hat to her husband, as a sign that she acknowledged his authority to the last, and her shoes and stockings to Anne, her daughter, in the hope that she would follow in her mother's footsteps. Anne afterwards became a nun.

Margaret was to be pressed to death immediately. In their eagerness to kill her the persecutors had dispensed with the preliminary three-day torture. Inside the Tolbooth the executioners were waiting—ragged tramps, male and female, hired for a few pence.

Before she lay down the persecutors demanded that she pray with them. "I will not pray with you, and you shall not pray with me," Margaret told them, "neither

will I say Amen to your prayers, nor shall you to
mine."

One humiliation she was spared. While the women
stood around her, she was allowed to change into a
short linen dress which she had made especially for
her execution. To the sleeves she had sewn tapes with
which, when she had stretched herself on the ground,
they tied her hands to two posts driven into the floor.
It was an honor, Margaret had declared, to die in the
same attitude as her Savior.

The heavy door was placed over her, and then the
weights. "Jesu, Jesu, Jesu, have mercy on me," she
cried out as the agony began. A pool of blood formed
slowly on the floor beside her, but she uttered no other
word. For 15 slow minutes the life was crushed out of
her. Then the terrible gasps ceased and Margaret
Clitherow was dead.

A year or so after Margaret Clitherow's death, the
congregation at the Bridewell Church in London received a rude shock as they offered up their Anglican
prayers on Sunday morning. From the pews stepped a
man still young, but whose face was already lined and
drawn with suffering. Eyes blazing, he faced them,
stopping the startled parson in midsentence.

"I have to tell all of you," he cried out in a loud
voice, "that I did very ill in coming lately to church
with you and joining in your service. For you call it the
service of God untruly—it is indeed the service of the
devil."

The man clearly had much more to say, but he did
not get the chance. Within seconds he had been
pulled to the ground by a scrimmage of outraged
worshippers, one of whom clapped a hand over his
mouth to stop any further blasphemy. Minutes later,

their prayers forgotten, the congregation were hauling Richard Watson through the streets to the nearby prison.

The Bridewell jail had its own torture cell, like the Tower of London's "little ease," where a man could neither stand upright nor stretch himself out to sleep. Into this Richard was thrust, loaded with irons, and fed for a month on just enough bread and water to keep alive.

Starved and ill, seeing no face but that of the scowling jailer who brought his rations, Richard nevertheless felt at peace. He was now making amends for that terrible day when he, a Catholic priest, had given way to his tormentors in this very prison and taken part in the Protestant service.

The priest hunters had released him then, and the triumphant smiles on their faces had haunted him in the days which followed, days in which he knew the inner torments of Judas. Unlike Judas Richard did not despair; he went to a prison where he knew fellow priests were held, confessed his apostasy, and received absolution.

That he might have been tailed to the prison worried Richard not at all, for he was determined to renounce Protestantism as publicly as he had embraced it. He knew very well the price that he would have to pay, and he now paid it gladly.

After a month of starvation he was moved to a bigger cell on the prison's top floor, where at least he had light and air and where the food was a little better. Here the Protestant ministers did their best to make the weakened man turn his coat once more. If only he would pretend to be a Protestant, they coaxed, he could believe what he liked inwardly. Threats, promises, argument—they tried everything. This time they had no success, though their efforts so wearied Richard that he wished that he could die to escape from their clutches.

If only a Catholic friend could visit him to utter a word of encouragement! It would be the best antidote to this mental torture. No use to hope for that, Richard told himself. The local Catholics would keep away lest they be accused of seducing him back to Rome.

He was not abandoned. In the city outside one person, at least, was anxiously trying to figure out a way to help him. Her name was Margaret Ward.

We know tantalizingly little about Margaret's background, merely that she came from Congleton, in Cheshire, and was herself a gentlewoman. At the time Richard Watson was arrested she was employed in the London household of "a lady of the first rank." Who this exalted lady was or what position Margaret filled in her house we are not told. Evidently she was a Catholic, for when Margaret asked permission to visit the jailed priest it was readily given.

Did Margaret already know Richard? Was she one of those to whom he had ministered before his arrest? Again we do not know. We know only that she changed her dress, presumably so that she would not look like a servant, and set out for the Bridewell determined to see him at all costs.

Over her arm she carried a basket of food, which she asked permission to take inside to the priest. As she had fully expected, she met with a blunt refusal. Soon she was back on the same errand. Although she had no more success than before, she stopped to chat with the jailer's wife, who obviously liked her and was perhaps flattered to find herself on friendly terms with one so obviously a lady.

The 18th-century Bishop Challoner, having already told his readers the story of Margaret Clitherow, quaintly calls Margaret Ward "a gentlewoman with a courage above her sex." It was not only courage that Margaret had in common with her York namesake. She had charm, will power, and a fair share of feminine guile, and she used them all to become a saint.

Before long she had got the jailer's wife firmly on her side. Her friend used her own charm on her husband and Margaret was grudgingly given permission to see Richard, provided that she submitted to a search before each visit. Searched she was, so thoroughly that even the loaves and pies in her basket were broken open to make sure that no message was hidden inside.

At first she was never allowed to be alone with Richard. After a month, however, Margaret won even the jailer's confidence and the security restrictions were relaxed.

Margaret's calm, smiling face, the whispered news of friends outside, the assurance of prayers, the good food which she brought him, all worked together to make a new man of Richard. Gone now was his despair, his wish to die. With the jailer out of earshot, he leaned forward and whispered that he was planning to escape.

He could force the cell window, he was sure of that. But outside was a sheer drop of 50 or 60 feet. If he was to get out, he would need a rope.

Swiftly Margaret went to work. Taking two Catholic watermen into her confidence, she asked them to be ready with their boat at a point where the river ran close to the prison, at between two and three o'clock the following morning. As soon as Richard let himself down they were to row him swiftly away through the darkness to the safety of a friend's home.

Heart pounding, Margaret arrived at the prison with her basket, trying to seem as normal as possible as she

paused for her accustomed chat with the jailer's wife.
For weeks now they had made no attempt to search
her. Would they suddenly decide to do so this time?

The jailer appeared with his usual gruff greeting and
led the way upstairs. Margaret breathed again. There
was to be no search. If her luck held, she should be
able to slip the rope to Richard without arousing
suspicion.

As soon as the door was locked behind them Margaret rummaged swiftly under the food, produced the
rope and assured Richard that the watermen would be
waiting. When the jailer returned, Richard was plac-
idly digging into a large meat pie.

That evening was the longest of Richard's life. He
wanted desperately to get out of the jail, not because he
feared anything that his enemies might do to him, but
because he was eager to get back to work as a priest.
He could not stay in London, he knew that. Once he
was on the outside the city would be too hot to hold
him; he would be the most wanted man in London.
No, he would have to head for some other part of the
country where his face was not known.

Midnight came at last, then one o'clock. Richard
prayed and listened, "Please, God, let the escape
succeed, but whatever the outcome, may your will be
done."

At last two o'clock struck. Already Richard had
worked on the window latch and now it gave easily as
he forced it down. The authorities, figuring that no
prisoner could drop 50 feet, had never troubled to
make it escape proof.

Outside and above the window was a protruding
cornice. Climbing onto the ledge, Richard hung his
doubled rope carefully over it, making sure that it
would not slip. Then, holding both ends, he began to
climb down the wall like a descending mountaineer.

When he reached the ground he would pull the rope down after him. The jailer must not find it—he would guess at once who had smuggled it into the prison.

Suddenly his descent ceased. Both ends of the rope tightened in his hands. Bewildered, he glanced upwards into the darkness and then down at the ground below him. With a sickening jolt he realized that there had been a terrible mistake. *The rope was too short.*

It was his fault, Richard told himself bitterly. He should have made it clear that he would need a rope stretching double the distance from the window to the ground. Yet, surely, he *had* made it clear. Margaret must have underestimated the length.

It was useless to wonder who was to blame. Dangling helplessly 20 feet above the ground, he realized that he had no choice but to let himself fall.

With a silent prayer Richard put his safety in God's keeping and released his hold on one end of the rope. The watermen, waiting nearby, heard a sickening crash as his body, falling through the darkness, crashed on to the roof of a shed which stood beneath the prison wall.

They found him, stunned and moaning, lying across the splintered roof. He had fallen awkwardly; an arm and a leg, twisted under him, had both been broken.

The noise of his fall had aroused those inside the prison. Already they could hear voices. In a moment, men with lanterns would be on the scene. With no time to lose, one of the men clambered on to the roof and eased the injured priest into his colleague's arms.

It took only a moment to reach the boat, for the thin, suffering body was no great weight. Laying Richard gently in the bottom they seized their oars and pulled away up the dark river.

Until now Richard has been semiconscious, but the

cold night air revived him. As he came to his senses a sickening realization made him struggle upright.

"The rope," he murmured. "If they find the rope, they'll know it was Mrs. Ward who brought it in."

On the riverbank behind them they could already hear shouts and see lantern rays. The hue and cry was in full swing. Almost certainly, the rope had been found already.

"Lie down again," urged one of the watermen in an Irish brogue. "We'll warn the lady to fly."

The warning came too late. The pursuivants came for Margaret just as she was about to slip from the house to a hiding place across the city.

In prison they loaded her with chains and kept her for eight days in solitary confinement. Steadfastly she refused to tell them Richard's whereabouts. They flogged her, then they hung her by the wrists, with only the tips of her toes touching the ground, for so long that she was crippled. Still Margaret would not speak. Her sufferings were, she said, but a prelude to the martyrdom with which she hoped to be honored.

The priest hunters never did catch Richard, who slowly recovered and then disappeared to minister outside London. They did, however, make another arrest.

John Roche, the Irish waterman, had changed clothes with the injured priest to help him evade capture when he moved on. A few days later, walking in the street, he was spotted by the jailer, who at once recognized the clothes in which his prisoner had escaped. So John joined Margaret behind bars.

Eight days later Margaret Ward faced her judges. Had she, they demanded, been guilty of helping a priest to escape?

"I have never in my life done anything of which I less repented than the delivering of that innocent lamb from those bloody wolves," she replied calmly.

They tried once more to frighten her into betraying Richard's whereabouts, but soon saw that they were wasting their time. Passing the inevitable death sentence, they told her that the queen was merciful and that she could escape hanging if she would ask pardon and go to church.

"I have never offended Her Majesty, and it is not just to confess a fault by asking for pardon where there is none," declared Margaret. "As to what I did in favoring the priest's escape, I believe that the queen herself, if she had the bowels of a woman, would have done as much if she had known the suffering which he was undergoing."

Bluntly she told them that she would never go against her conscience by attending the Protestant church, and so they might hang her if they pleased.

"Death for such a cause would be very welcome to me," she added. "I would willingly lay down not one life, but many, if I had them, rather than act against my duty to God and his holy religion."

On August 30, 1588, Margaret Ward was hanged along with John Roche, a priest named Richard Leigh, and three other laymen: Edward Shelley, Richard Martin and Richard Flower, all condemned of helping priests. They sang on their way to Tyburn.

5
Topcliffe's Victims

Hurrying along the east side of St. Paul's Cathedral, Edmund Gennings stopped suddenly. A strange feeling had taken hold of him: he trembled as though terrified, his hair stood on end, his body was bathed in sweat. In constant danger, he knew of nothing which should make him, at that moment, feel especially afraid.

Was he about to be arrested? Had some unknown instinct warned him of it even before the hand descended on his shoulder?

Bracing himself, he turned and looked behind. The street was empty, save for a young man in a brown cloak some distance away.

Clearly the youth intended him no harm. Indeed, he did not seem to have noticed Edmund's presence. With a sigh of relief the young priest hurried on to the house where he was to say Mass.

Still only 23, Edmund had been ordained in France a few months previously and had set out for England in disguise almost at once. Born at Lichfield, in Staffordshire, he had been a Protestant until, at the age of 16, he went as a page into the household of a Catholic gentleman named Richard Sherwood.

His master's fine qualities, springing so obviously from his faith, made Edmund decide that he, too, would become a Catholic. When Mr. Sherwood went abroad to study for the priesthood, his young page soon followed.

The youngster's fervor so much impressed the college authorities that they obtained Rome's permission for him to be ordained below the canonical age. At one time it had looked as though an attack of tuberculosis might stop him from being ordained at all, but he was cured suddenly by what may well have been a miracle.

Edmund travelled to England with two other new priests, Alexander Rawlins and Hugo Sewel. Alexander, too, was destined for martyrdom; he was executed at York five years later.

On their journey through France the three were arrested by Huguenots, thrown into Abbeville prison, ill treated and threatened with death. Released and run out of town, they set sail from Treport, in Normandy, and landed by night at Whitby, a little Yorkshire fishing port, after their boat had almost been smashed to pieces against the cliffs.

Ashore lay still more danger. In a Whitby inn they aroused the suspicion of a priest catcher named Ratcliffe, who questioned them closely before allowing them to go on their way.

After six months in the North Edmund set out for Lichfield in the hope of converting his family and friends. He arrived to find that most of them were dead. John, the younger brother whom he had last seen more than eight years before, was now leading a dissolute life in London. So to London Edmund went, determined to find John and do whatever he could to save his soul.

For many days he searched, but nobody in the capital seemed even to have heard of his brother. In the end he gave up hope and prepared to head back north. Sad and disappointed, he had almost forgotten the strange incident near St. Paul's.

Then it happened again. This time he was walking along Ludgate Hill, on the other side of the cathedral, when the same symptoms attacked him. He turned and saw a young man in a brown cloak.

This time Edmund stared hard. Could this possibly be his brother? John had been a small boy when last Edmund had seen him. By now he would be about the age of this man. And the face . . . As he saw it clearly, Edmund felt sure that his search had ended.

"Forgive me for asking, my friend," said Edmund as the young man approached, "but from what part of the country do you come?"

"From Lichfield, in Staffordshire," replied the youngster, looking at Edmund curiously.

"And your name?"

"Gennings."

Edmund's heart raced. How he longed to throw his arms around the lad, to tell him who he was! But that would be folly at this stage. Sticking to his previously chosen alias, he told John that his own name was Ironmonger and that they were kinsmen. Cautiously, he asked after John's brother, Edmund. The youngster's brow darkened.

"I hear that my brother has become a popish priest and a traitor, and that if he is caught he will certainly be hanged," he declared.

"Indeed?" replied Edmund with a smile. "I have heard quite differently. I have heard that he is a very honest man, who loves both his queen and his country, but who loves God above all."

Now he could see recognition dawning in his brother's eyes.

"Tell me, good cousin John," he continued quietly, "would you not know your brother if you were to see him?"

"I believe that I should now, for I believe that you are he."

As Edmund opened his mouth to speak, John raised a warning hand. His young face was grim.

"If you are indeed Edmund," he declared, "then let me tell you that you will bring very great discredit upon me and my friends if you attempt to associate with us."

"But my dear John, my dear, dear brother . . . ."

"No, Edmund," John interrupted. His expression was grimmer still. "In your religion I will never follow you. Never!"

The sadness in his older brother's eyes sent a sudden, unexpected stab through the boy's heart.

"In everything else, though," he added gently, "I will always respect you—very much."

He turned away. Edmund had a hand on his arm. "At least tell me where I can find you again," he begged.

John hesitated. "Ask for me at the sign of the Three Feathers," he said at last. Then he was gone.

Edmund walked on down Ludgate Hill with a light heart. Though he had to leave for the present he would soon be back, and he would not rest until he had won John away from his gambling and drinking, and shown him the way to the true Church. If necessary, he would follow him to the Three Feathers and to every low tavern in town.

To London Edmund returned, but he never saw

John again. On the morning after his arrival, he and a priest friend, Polydore Plasden, met to say Mass in Gray's Inn Fields, at a house belonging to a bluff Catholic gentleman named Swithun Wells.

As Edmund uttered the words of consecration there was a loud hammering at the door below and harsh voices demanded that they open in the name of the queen. A second later the door crashed inwards and the footsteps of bawling, cursing men clattered up the stairs to the Mass room.

Brian Lacy rushed to the door, with John Mason and Sydney Hodgson at his heels. All three were laymen, young and strong. Facing them at the top of the stairs was a man whose cruel mouth and staring eyes they recognized at once. Of all priest catchers Richard Topcliffe was the most notorious and the most savage, a psychopath who sometimes tortured prisoners in his own home.

"Stand back, you popish villains!" roared Topcliffe. The three Catholics promptly flung him down the stairs.

With a roar Topcliffe picked himself up and prepared to charge back, yelling at the gang behind him to follow. Three drawn swords stopped him in his tracks.

From the doorway behind the three young men stepped Polydore Plasden, himself still in his twenties. He looked at Topcliffe steadily.

"If you will wait below until we have finished the Mass," he said quietly, "we will surrender and come with you."

Topcliffe looked again at the sharp sword points. "So be it," he snarled.

Sheathing their swords, the three followed Polydore back into the room. The Blessed Sacrament was safe from profane hands; nothing else mattered.

Edmund completed the Mass as carefully and reverently as though nothing were wrong and all received Holy Communion. Then they went downstairs to the hall where Topcliffe and his gang were waiting.

Swithun Wells was not among them, for he had been out of town when the Mass was arranged.

Returning to find his home ransacked and his wife in jail, he strode into the office of Judge Yonge and demanded her release. Within minutes Swithun himself was under arrest, with a pair of iron bolts on his legs.

In Newgate prison next day the two men faced each other once more. Yonge demanded to know whether Swithun had been present at the Mass. Swithun replied that he had not and that he very much regretted it. "So, you missed the feast," observed Yonge dryly. "Never mind, you shall taste of the sauce."

Before moving to London, Swithun had run a private school in Wiltshire from which came many future priests, some of whom were martyred. Now he was going to follow in his pupils' footsteps.

At the trial Edmund Gennings argued the Catholic case so vigorously that the irritated judges could only respond with more sneers. When these failed they descended to outright buffoonery, dressing Edmund in a jester's multicolored coat which had been found in Swithun's house.

Polydore Plasden, too, came in for his share of judicial wit. When the jury brought in the inevitable verdict, he told the Bench, "These 12 simple men find us guilty of treason for exercising our priestly function. But you, learned in the law and in history, know quite well that the priestly function was in all ages an honorable calling."

Fleetwood, the recorder of London, know that Polydore's father kept a musical instrument shop.

"Plasden, dost thou talk so?" he answered. "Methinks thou wouldst better wind a horn, for I think thy father is a horner at Fleet Bridge." Dutiful titters greeted this polished sally.

Of the ten people present at the Mass in Swithun's house, nine suffered martyrdom together with Swithun himself. Mrs. Wells, to her great sorrow, was reprieved at the last moment and died in prison more than ten years later.

December 10, 1591, was a busy day for Richard Topcliffe. While Polydore and others were taken to Tyburn, Edmund and Swithun were to die in Gray's Inn Fields, opposite Swithun's front door. Topcliffe had to attend both executions.

As Edmund stood under the gallows Topcliffe urged him to confess his "treason" while there was still time. Edmund replied with so much spirit that the priest catcher flew into a rage. Moments later, he took a terrible revenge.

Barely had the cart been driven away and the rope tightened round his neck than Topcliffe ordered the hangman to cut him down. As Edmund dropped to the ground the man tripped him so that he fell, still fully conscious, across the disembowelling block.

Feeling the knife rip into his body, he screamed in agony. Swithun, who would be spared the butchery, encouraged the young priest just as Richard Reynolds had comforted his fellow martyrs nearly 60 years before.

As the executioner reached for his heart, Edmund called on Saint Gregory to pray for him.

"His heart is in my hand," cried the man, "and Gregory is upon his lips!"

All his life Swithun Wells had been a cheerful extrovert, a cultured man whose favorite recreations were outdoor. On his journey to Tyburn he had spotted in the crowd an old companion of the sporting field. "Farewell, dear friend!" he called gaily. "Farewell all hawking, hunting, and old pastimes! I am now going a better way."

On the very brink of death his high spirits did not desert him. Shivering in the winter air, he urged Topcliffe to get on with the execution. "Despatch, Mr. Topcliffe, despatch," he cried. "Are you not ashamed to suffer an old man to stand here so long in his shirt in the cold?"

And so Swithun Wells, like Thomas More before him, died with a joke on his lips, expressing the hope that the priest catcher would turn from Saul to Paul and become a good Catholic. So far as we know, his prayer was not answered.

At Tyburn, where Topcliffe now hurried, one of his victims almost slipped through his fingers. As he stood in the cart, Polydore Plasden was heard to pray aloud for the sovereign, as did most martyrs before and after him.

Sir Walter Raleigh, the great explorer and man of letters, was among the spectators who heard the "traitor" ask God to bless Elizabeth.

"Dost thou think in the same sense in which thou prayest?" he asked astonished.

"Yes," Polydore replied, "otherwise I could expect no salvation."

"Dost thou acknowledge her for thy lawful queen?"

"Yes."

"Wouldst thou defend her against foreign enemies, if thou wert able?"

"Yes, and so I would counsel all men."

His replies brought the crowd firmly on to Polydore's side.

"There is no cause why this honest man should die," someone shouted. A roar of approval greeted the words.

"Mr. Sheriff, let him be stayed," commanded Raleigh. "I will go at once to the court."

Raleigh's downfall and death on the block were still in the future. He had the ear of the queen and he would use his influence on Polydore's side. But Topcliffe was not to be robbed of his prey now, even by Sir Walter Raleigh.

"Plasden," the harsh voice rang out, "dost thou think that the queen hath any right to maintain this religion and to forbid yours?"

"No."

"Then thou thinkest not to defend the queen against the Pope, if he would come to establish thy religion?"

"I am a Catholic priest, therefore I would never fight, nor counsel others to fight, against my religion, for that were to deny my faith," replied Polydore. Looking up to heaven, he kissed the rope with which they were about to hang him.

"O Christ, I will never deny thee for a thousand lives," he declared.

Raleigh bit his lip. Nothing, he knew, could save Polydore now. Yet one thing more he could do.

"Let him hang till he be dead, Mr. Sheriff," he begged.

The sheriff nodded. When Polydore was cut down and the butchery began, it was upon a corpse that the hangman wielded his knife.

Eustace White, who also died at Tyburn that day, was a Lincolnshire man born at Louth. Like so many of our martyrs he was a convert. When he became a Catholic, his Protestant father laid a solemn curse on him. Evidently it did not work, for he did well in his studies in France and at the English College in Rome, and was ordained priest in 1588.

For three years he worked in the West of England, dodging the priest hunters successfully until he chanced to fall into the company of a traveller who was riding in the same direction as himself. His companion was, it turned out, a lawyer. From the tone of his conversation, Eustace gathered that he was sympathetic to the Catholic religion. Soon the young priest was speaking more frankly than he would normally have done to a total stranger.

When they reached Blandford, in Dorset, his new friend pressed Eustace to have breakfast with him at an inn. And there he was arrested, betrayed by the man whom he had trusted.

As soon as it was established that Eustace was indeed a priest, the usual Protestant minister was summoned in an effort to win him from Rome.

Soon the two men were arguing briskly, about what particular point of dogma we are unfortunately not told. Eustace quoted a Scripture passage which the minister, a certain Dr. Howell, declared did not exist.

"That passage is in your own Bible," declared Eustace.

"It is not," answered Howell, a man noted for his learning.

"Bring me a Protestant Bible," Eustace told him, "and if I cannot find the passage there I will go with you to the Protestant church."

"If you can show it to me," Howell retorted, "I will become a papist."

News of the dispute spread round the town. Next day a crowd turned up to see the battle.

Howell turned up, complete with Bible. Instead of handing it to Eustace, however, he kept it firmly tucked under his arm. At once he launched on an argument totally different from that of the previous day.

Eustace, not a man to be sidetracked, appealed to the crowd and tried to pluck the Bible from its resting place. Howell held on tight.

Seizing the initiative, Eustace let Howell retire discomfited and warned the crowd that false doctrine was seducing them from the true faith. So persuasively did he speak that even some of Blandford's staunchest Protestants voted him the most learned man in England.

Some of his hearers wanted to petition the queen for his release, but that was not to be. Taken to London, he was delivered to the mercy of Topcliffe and tortured seven times in an effort to make him betray other Catholics. Once he was hung up by the hands in iron manacles for eight hours, the sweat soaking his clothes and forming a pool on the ground beneath him. He uttered only a prayer, "Lord, more pain if Thou pleasest, and more patience."

When he recovered, he told Topcliffe that he felt no anger towards him, but that he would pray for him because he needed prayers.

"I do not want the prayers of a traitor," roared Topcliffe, "and I'll have you hanged at the next sessions."

"Then I will pray for you, sir, at the foot of the gallows, for you have great need of prayers," replied Eustace. And he kept his word.

Finally, what of John Gennings, the young ne'er-do-well with whom Edmund was reunited so briefly? Not only did he ignore his brother's trial and execution but, as he later admitted, he actually felt relieved at the news. Now Edmund would trouble him no more—or so he thought.

Ten days after Edmund's death he returned home from a day of drinking and gambling to find himself suddenly seized by a wave of depression. Try as he might, he could not get Edmund out of his mind; he compared his own life with his brother's and felt bitterly ashamed.

His body shaking with sobs, he begged God to show him a better way and, although he had never done so before, he began to pray fervently to our Lady and the saints. As he prayed he had a strong sense that Edmund was near. He even thought that he could see him and hear his voice.

There and then John Gennings made a vow to find out the truth about the Catholic religion. Without a word to his friends he went abroad and eventually became a student at Douai. Ordained in 1607, he returned as a secular priest to England. After several years' work he went back to France, became a Franciscan and returned once more to his homeland to reestablish the Order there, becoming the first English provincial since the Reformation.

6
Drama in the Dock

The sour-faced earl of Huntingdon did not smile
often, but he was smiling now. Before him, manacled
and surrounded by armed guards, stood the most
hunted man in the North of England. For 13 years
John Boste had dodged Huntingdon's pursuivants.
Now he was caught, "one of the greatest stags in the
forest," the earl called him triumphantly.

Smugly, the captors awaited their chief's congratulations. The earl delivered a long-winded speech prais-
ing their efforts. He had never doubted, he said, that
one day these would be rewarded. When he had
finished, the prisoner managed a wry grin.

"And after all this long search, my lord, you have got
your boast," he observed. How the joke went down we
are not told.

Doomed though he might be, John could better
afford to smile than the Puritan nobleman. For John
Boste knew that after his death others would come to
carry on his work, and more still after them. Hun-

tingdon, sent north to stamp out Catholicism, might as well try to stop the wind from blowing across the fields.

Born at Penrith, Cumberland, John had taken an M.A. degree at Oxford before enrolling in the Douai seminary at its new home at Rheims. Returning as a priest to his native North country, he used his strong personality and his warm sense of humor to win converts and bring back waverers. This, with his talent for keeping one jump ahead of the pursuers, caused much anger and frustration to Huntingdon and his Council of the North.

Of course John knew that he would be caught one day. In the end, like Edmund Campion and John Payne, he was betrayed by a Judas. This one was named Francis Ecclesfield, a renegade Catholic who, having gone sacrilegiously to confession and Holy Communion, promptly told the priest catchers where they could lay hands on the notorious Father Boste. At Waterhouses, a few miles from Durham, they found him hiding in a specially constructed "priest's hole" in the house where he had said Mass.

Dismissed from Huntingdon's presence, he was taken south to London and the Tower. There he was racked so viciously that he was permanently crippled. Needless to say, the torturers got nothing out of him.

Back in Durham he faced the usual farce of a trial. With him in the dock were a fellow priest, John Ingram, and a former lay reader named George Swallowell who, becoming convinced that the Catholic faith was the true faith, had boldly said so from his Anglican pulpit.

After a year in Durham jail, however, poor George was beginning to weaken. Sentenced to the customary cruel death, he lost courage completely and consented to return to the Church of England.

"Swallowell, what has thou done?"

Turning his head, George looked into the calm, unafraid eyes of John Boste. For a moment he was confused, but only for a moment. Getting a grip on himself, he begged Huntingdon to let him speak once more.

Realizing that John was about to snatch his prey from him, the earl tried to hold on.

"Swallowell," he warned, "look well what thou doest, for although thou be condemned, yet the queen is merciful."

George was adamant. He wanted to address the court once more.

Huntingdon stared at the tormented man with hard eyes. If the fellow chose to die, then let him.

"If thou be so earnest," he said slowly, "thou shalt have thy word again. Say what thou wilt."

George drew himself up.

"In the faith in which these two priests do die, I also will die," he declared, "and the faith which they profess, I also profess."

"You would have laughed," a bystander recorded, "to hear the mutterings of the court at this."

Delightedly, John laid a hand on his friend's head.

"Hold thee there, Swallowell," he cried, "and my soul for thine!"

This was too much for the earl.

"Away with Boste—he is reconciling him!" he yelled, only just remembering to pass sentence before John was dragged out of his sight.

To achieve the maximum terror, the three executions were spread out across the northeast of England. John died at Durham on July 24, 1594, suffering the greatest possible cruelty but praying for the executioner. So strongly was the crowd on his side that a special guard was posted round the gallows.

John Ingram died at Newcastle on the following day and George Swallowell a day later, steadfast to the end despite the efforts which the officials made to terrify him into fresh apostasy. "I renounce all heresy," he said as he climbed the ladder, and he asked all Catholics present to pray for him.

7
Poet and Prince

The gypsy had laid her plans carefully. She knew just where little Robert slept and when she would find the nursery unattended. Creeping into the house at precisely the right moment, she took the sleeping baby from the cradle, slipped her own child in his place, and made her exit. With luck, no one would notice the substitution.

The gypsy's dream of having her own child brought up a gentleman were quickly dashed. Robert's nurse returned, took one look into the cradle, and the hue and cry was on. Soon Robert was safely back home and the gypsy behind bars.

It was an exciting start to a life which was to be exciting and much more besides. Robert Southwell, born at Horsham St. Faith in Norfolk, is possibly the best known of all the Forty Martyrs; not only a canonized saint but a poet whose reputation has stood the test of four centuries. His mother, related to a Sussex family called Shelley, forms a link between Robert and a later poet of very different beliefs.

Sent to Douai for his education, Robert decided early that he wanted to become a priest and a Religious. Hovering between the Carthusians and the Jesuits, he eventually chose the Society of Jesus only to find that it did not choose him. At 17, the father general ruled, young Master Southwell was too young to be accepted.

"Alas where am I, and where shall I be?" he wrote mournfully. "A wanderer in a dry and parched land."

Sensitive and scrupulous though he was, Robert was not the sort of youngster to go on moping. Having shown his spirit by walking to Rome, he was accepted even though he had not yet celebrated his 18th birthday. A brilliant student, he was ordained at 24 and was promptly made prefect of studies at the English College, where young men eager to sacrifice their own lives sang a *Te Deum* whenever news reached Rome that one of their number had been martyred.

The youthful professor wanted nothing more than to follow the same path. A year later, his wish was granted.

Before taking ship for the secret crossing, he sent a farewell letter to his best friend, a Flemish Jesuit called John Deckers. "It is true that the flesh is weak and can do nothing, and even now revolts from that which is proposed," he wrote. "Yet God who is mighty will be at my right hand lest I be shaken."

Torn between Carthusian solitude and the Jesuit front line, Robert Southwell had made his choice. Now he craved martyrdom, the chance had come— and he was terrified. Yet never for a moment did he think of drawing back.

Arriving at London Bridge in the dawn, he saw the pikes with their severed heads rising through the morning mist like a crown of thorns. Soon he was at the house of Lord Vaux, the Catholic peer who was to give him shelter. The whole family quickly took the handsome, gifted young priest to their hearts.

Throughout his short life Robert gave his affection freely and received it in full measure from others. His Jesuit colleagues, men not noted for effusiveness, wrote with special warmth to "dear Brother Robert." Henry Garnet, a fellow martyr, called him "prudent, pious, meek and exceedingly winning." His gentleness drew men and women alike, and it reaches us through his poems, especially those dedicated to the infant Jesus:

> Behold, a silly tender Babe
> In freezing winter night
> In homely manger trembling lies
> Alas, a piteous sight!
>
> The inns are full; no man will yield
> This little pilgrim bed,
> But forced he is with silly beasts
> In crib to shroud his head.
>
> Despise him not for lying there,
> First, what he is inquire;
> An orient pearl is often found
> In depth of dirty mire.

That Robert was also brave and physically tough he showed both now and, even more so, later on. He had his full share of hair's-breadth escapes, especially at Baddesley Clinton, where the priest hunters raided the house at five in the morning just as he was about to begin Mass. He just had time to hide his Mass kit and climb into the hiding hole when they burst in.

A similar adventure, at Hackney, he describes himself: "I heard them threatening and breaking woodwork and sounding the walls to find hiding places; yet, by God's goodness, after four hours' search they found me not, though separated from them only by a thin partition rather than a wall."

In his role as a dashing Elizabethan gentleman Robert needed to know the hawking and hunting terms so frequently on the lips of the leisured class. Having spent most of his life abroad he was not familiar with them and relied for tuition upon Father John Gerard, a Jesuit colleague who has been well described as the leader of the Catholic underground. Father Gerard proved an able tutor, but poor Robert lived in terror of making a gaffe and so blowing his cover.

It was not merely to aid his disguise that Robert needed to play the sportsman. Hawking and hunting language proved useful in changing the subject when Protestant gentlemen indulged in smutty talk or began to abuse the Catholic Church.

During most of his six-year ministry in London Robert was based at Arundel House, just off the Strand. This was the home of Anne, countess of Arundel, whose husband was already in the Tower for his religion. Though the two men were never to meet, Robert's smuggled letters strengthened the earl during his long ordeal.

Other men of rank were among his many converts, or among those he reconciled to the Church. Despite his difficulties with the sporting terms, Robert moved easily among the upper class. The more converts he gained, the higher he rose on Topcliffe's "wanted" list.

Living constantly with danger, he found a new maturity. No longer did he look forward overeagerly to martyrdom, or feel the cold hand of fear. Though men like Topcliffe remained implacable in their hatred, at times, he noted, the general public seemed to experi-

ence something akin to shame at the treatment meted
out to those whose only crime was their loyalty to the
old faith:

"A month or two ago things were being done against
the Catholics that only the filth of heresy could have
conceived. But now this horrid cruelty has fallen back
upon itself, and though it has not ceased to be cruelty,
yet there are degrees of cruelty which make it able to
blush at itself."

In *Time Goes by Turns* he filters the experience
which he has gained through his own poetic consciousness:

Not always fall of leaf, nor ever Spring,
No endless night, yet not eternal day:
The saddest birds a season find to sing,
The roughest storm a calm may soon allay.
Thus with succeeding turns God tempereth all
That man may hope to rise yet fear to fall.

Like so many other martyrs Robert Southwell was
betrayed, though this time one can only feel pity for
the betrayer. Anne Bellamy was the daughter of a
Middlesex family in whose house Robert had said
Mass. Arrested by Topcliffe, she entered prison determined to suffer for her faith. Three months later she
was broken: Topcliffe had raped her and in consequence she was pregnant.

When he heard the news the culprit himself grew
fearful, for the queen frowned on sexual immorality.
The old lecher had to redeem himself quickly, and he
resolved that Anne herself should be the means of his
doing so.

Topcliffe was now in his sixties, but he promised
Anne that he would marry her off to a personable
young husband if she would help him to catch
Robert Southwell. The bridegroom-elect was Nicholas
White, another of the torturer's minions and the son of

a weaver. For him, marriage to Anne would be a step up the social ladder. In her distraught state Anne agreed, and the trap was set.

Receiving an urgent message from the unhappy girl, Robert assumed that she wished to go to confession and rode at once to Uxenden Hall, the family home. At midnight Topcliffe and his men surrounded the house. When he strode inside he was brandishing a plan which showed the precise location of the priest's hiding hole.

Robert, who could hear everything, emerged and confronted the torturer calmly. Topcliffe, nonplussed, turned from the terrified family.

"Who are you?" demanded Topcliffe of the handsome figure before him.

"A gentleman," replied Robert, looking him in the eyes. Topcliffe replied with a stream of epithets.

"Sir, these are hard words," Robert told him. "By what right do you use them?"

"Priest! Traitor! *Jesuit!*" yelled Topcliffe.

At Topcliffe's house in Westminster Robert was tortured ten times, being hung by his wrists for as long as seven hours at a time, with his ankles tied to his thighs. Round each wrist was a sharp circle of iron pressing on the artery.

"I never did take so weighty a man, if he be rightly used," Topcliffe had written gleefully to the queen. Though he would have preferred death to the torture he endured, Robert told his tormentor nothing. Altogether he spent three years in prison, part of the time in the Tower, where he was tortured three times more.

At his trial the attorney general, Sir Edward Coke, set out to prove that the Jesuits were professional liars who taught others their mendacious ways. Was it not true, he demanded, that Robert had taught Anne Bellamy that she might deny on oath that she had seen a priest at her father's house, even if she had done so, on the ground that she had not seen him with intent to betray him?

Robert replied that mental reservations of this kind were entirely in accord with Scripture and the Fathers. Furthermore, he declared, it would be impossible to preserve the security of the state without them.

Suppose, he argued, that England were invaded by the French, and the queen forced to hide in a private house—a hiding place known only to the attorney general. If the attorney, under interrogation, refused to swear that she was not there, would that not be tantamount to betraying the sovereign?

In vain did Sir Edward and the judges try to knock down his argument. When he fielded their objections, they could only reply with abuse.

Because public feeling was so much on Robert's side, the government tried to keep the date of his execution secret. To divert attention from Tyburn they had a notorious highwayman executed elsewhere at the same time.

Word got around just the same and a huge crowd gathered to see him die. His speech from the scaffold must surely have been one of the most dignified and moving ever heard at that bloody spot:

> "I am come hither to play out the last act of this poor life. . . . I do profess myself to be a Catholic priest of the Holy Roman Church, and of the Society of Jesus, and I do thank God eternally for it. . . . This is my death, my last farewell to this unfortunate life, and yet to me most happy and most fortunate. I pray it may be for the full satisfaction of my sins, for the good of my country, and for the comfort of many others. Which death, albeit that it seem here disgraceful, yet I hope that in time to come it will be to my eternal glory."

It is unlikely that anyone in that vast crowd wanted to see Robert Southwell suffer the sentence in all its barbarity. When the sheriff signed to the hangman to cut him down, there was a swift objection from one of the noblemen at the front of the crowd. So Robert hung until he was dead. When his head was struck off and displayed, not a single voice was heard to cry "traitor." And the hangman, when he carried the lifeless body to the quartering block, did so reverently—a thing never seen at Tyburn before.

For much of his imprisonment Robert had been kept in a cell only a few yards from that of Philip Howard, earl of Arundel, the friend whom he never met. When Robert became Anne's chaplain at Arundel House, Philip was already in the Tower. He was to stay there for 11 long years.

Nobody, at the beginning of his career, would have predicted a martyr's crown for Philip. Brought up a Protestant, as a teenager he saw his father, the duke of Norfolk, executed for plotting to marry Mary, Queen of Scots.

"Beware of the court," the duke had warned his son in a farewell message. Philip ignored the advice. Plunging into that glittering world, he became a favorite of the queen who had beheaded his father; a playboy who neglected his young Catholic wife and was unfaithful to her.

The shallowness of his life soon made him unhappy, however, and he actually talked things over secretly with a Catholic priest. Though nothing came of the meeting, Philip's unhappiness continued.

The turning point came when he joined the audience at the debate between Edmund Campion and the Anglican theologians. Listening as the doomed Jesuit trounced his persecutors, Philip knew he had to become a Catholic.

It was no easy decision, for he would certainly lose his place at court and perhaps bring even worse trouble on his head. For a time he tried to stifle his conscience in a round of games and parties, but grace proved too strong. The court saw him less and less as he made up to Anne for the hurt which he had inflicted on her. Soon a baby was on the way.

Resenting the loss of her favorite, the queen reacted cruelly by taking Anne from her home and keeping her under house arrest while the baby was born. Philip had the little girl baptized a Protestant and named her Elizabeth.

For the moment his nerve had failed, but the mood did not last long. A few months later, he became a Catholic.

Feeling himself threatened and uncertain what course to take, Philip wrote for advice to William Allen at Douai. Government agents, intercepting the letter, forged a reply suggesting that he flee the country.

Arrested on the high seas, he was brought back to England and lodged in the Tower. Here Elizabeth refused to let him see his wife and daughter, and when Anne bore him a son and heir the vindictive monarch had the news kept from him.

Tried on the usual trumped-up charges, Philip was sentenced to death during the Armada scare of 1588. Since he was a nobleman he expected to be beheaded as his father had been before him.

Yet the summons to the block never came. For year after year his imprisonment dragged on—years during which he spent long hours in prayer and bore patiently the separation from his wife and children.

Always fond of the open air, he was at first allowed a daily walk in the Tower grounds, but the privilege was withdrawn when crowds gathered to catch a glimpse of the popular young nobleman. Within the walls his only companions were a faithful manservant and a pet dog. One day the dog followed the lieutenant of the Tower on his rounds and so found its way to Robert Southwell's cell. When his pet returned, Philip remarked that he loved it all the more because it had met his friend.

Inevitably the years of imprisonment told on Philip's health. A few months after Robert's execution he fell suddenly ill at dinner. Though still only 38, he knew that he had not long to live.

He begged for one farewell visit from Anne and the children. Elizabeth replied that not only would she allow Philip to see them, she would restore him to his former position—if only he would abjure the Church of Rome. Sadly, Philip replied that he could not accept the condition.

Philip Howard died peacefully at noon on Sunday, October 19, 1595. Though his blood was not shed, he is numbered among the martyrs. On a fireplace in the Beauchamp Tower visitors may still read the Latin inscription which he carved there:

Quanto plus afflictionis pro Christo in hoc saeculo tanto plus gloriae cum Christo in futuro.

The more affliction for Christ in this world, the more glory for Christ in the future.

8
A Clear Case of Forgery

Among the crowd that watched Edmund Campion's execution was a young man named Henry Walpole, son of a Norfolk family and a Cambridge graduate who had come to London to study law. Henry, himself a Catholic, had gained a reputation at the university as a poet and wit, and now he seemed set for a successful career.

Silently he watched Edmund's body ripped open and cut into four quarters. With the deft insouciance of a butcher handling meat, the hangman flung the quarters into a huge pot of boiling water. When they were parboiled he would recover them so that they could be nailed up in four separate public places as a warning to other priests and to those who sheltered them.

Blood splashed crimson as the quarters went into the pot. Looking down, Henry saw that a spot of it had landed on his coat. In that moment the whole direction of his life changed. Seven months later, on July 7, 1582, the Douai register noted, "Mr. Henry Walpole has come to us from England; a discreet, grave and pious man."

From France he was sent to Rome to complete his studies for the priesthood and there, two years later, he entered the Society of Jesus. Three of his brothers—he came from a big family—were later to become Jesuits also.

Rome proving unsuitable for his health, Henry's superiors sent him to France, where he was ordained in 1588. The following year found him in the Netherlands, serving as a chaplain to the Spanish troops. There he was captured by the English, who kept him prisoner for a whole year until one of his brothers managed to obtain his release.

From the beginning Henry had longed to join the English mission, to carry on the work which Edmund Campion had helped to begin. To his huge disappointment, his superiors now sent him to Spain, where new seminaries for English students had been established at Seville and Valladolid. After spells teaching in both he was sent on to Flanders to help set up a new Jesuit school at St. Omer.

Obedient though he was, Henry continued to chafe. In England his fellow Jesuit, Father John Gerard, was carrying on a successful and dangerous mission. "Gerard doth much good, why not I?" he would often ask wistfully.

No doubt he feared that he was in for another bout of teaching, this time at St. Omer. He was wrong. Towards the end of 1593 the longed for instructions came. To England he was to go!

On the night of December 4, Henry and two companions landed at Flamborough Head on the Yorkshire coast. Less than 24 hours later, they were arrested.

What Henry Walpole felt as he was taken under guard to York we can only guess. He had expected to be caught sooner or later and he was fully prepared to die for his priesthood. Yet it must have seemed a cruel blow to fall into the hands of the enemy before he had said Mass or heard a single confession on English soil.

If Henry did feel disappointment or defeat, he soon overcame it. Suffering, rather than preaching, was to be his vocation. Very well, he would accept it joyfully. Who could tell what graces he might thus win for his fellow countrymen?

Brought before the earl of Huntingdon, he readily admitted that he was a priest and a Jesuit. Two months later, by order of the Privy Council, he was transferred to London.

Locked up in the Tower for a year, Henry Walpole was tortured no fewer than 14 times. The rack, the thumbscrew, the "scavenger's daughter" and the guantlet were all brought out in an effort to make him tell what he knew. The Jesuit superior in England, Father Henry Garnet, reported, "It is very well known how cruel any of those tortures are which are now in use. For it is a common thing to hang them up in the air six or seven hours by the hands and by means of certain irons, which hold their hands fast and cut them, they shed much blood in the torture."

A layman named James Atkinson had recently died after enduring this treatment, added Father Garnet. Nor was torture the only suffering which Henry had to undergo:

> "Blessed Father Walpole met in the Tower of London with the greatest misery and poverty, so that the lieutenant himself, though otherwise a hard-hearted and barbarous man, was moved to inquire after some of the Father's relations, and told them that he was in great and extraordinary want—without bed, without clothes, without anything to cover him, and that at a season when the cold was most sharp and piercing, so that himself, though an enemy, out of pure compassion had given him a little straw to sleep on."

During the long journey back to York for his trial, Henry never once slept in a bed but stretched out each night upon the ground. In York Castle, where he spent many days awaiting the arrival of the judges, his only bed was a mat three feet long on which he knelt to pray for the greater part of the night.

During this time he wrote a number of poems, including one upon the death of Edmund Campion. This attracted so much attention that the Catholic who published it was condemned by the Council of the North to lose his ears and to spend the rest of his days in prison.

At his own trial Henry defended himself with great vigor, despite all the suffering which he had undergone. Had he become a lawyer he would certainly have been a successful one, as we can judge from this exchange with Judge Beaumont, after Henry had argued that to be a priest could not in itself be treason.

Beaumont: Indeed the merely being a priest or a Jesuit is no treason; but what makes you a traitor is your returning into the kindom against the laws.

Henry: If to be a priest is no treason, the executing the office or doing the functions of a priest can be no treason.

Beaumont: But if a priest should conspire against the person of his prince, would not this be treason?

Henry: Yes, but then neither his being a priest nor the following the duties of his calling would make him a traitor, but the committing of a crime contrary to the duty of a priest, which is far from being my case.

Beaumont: You have been with the king of Spain and you have conversed with Parsons and Holt, and other rebels and traitors to the kingdom; and you have returned here contrary to the laws, and therefore you cannot deny your being a traitor.

Henry: To speak or treat with any person whatso-

ever out of the kingdom can make me no traitor, as
long as no proof can be brought that the subject about
which we treated was treason; neither can the returning to my native country be looked upon as treason,
since the cause of my return was not to do any evil,
either to the queen or to the kingdom.

Beaumont: Our laws appoint that a priest who
returns from beyond the seas and does not present
himself before a justice within three days to make the
usual submission to the queen's majesty in matters of
religion, shall be deemed a traitor.

Henry: Then I am out of the case, for I was apprehended before I had been one whole day upon English ground.

At which, the reporter records, Judge Beaumont was
"put to a nonplus."

Judge Elvin demanded that Henry there and then
submit to the queen's religious supremacy and abjure
the Pope. When Henry refused, the jury was directed
to find him guilty. Before they retired, Henry addressed them:

> "Gentlemen of the jury, I confess most willingly
> that I am a priest, and that I am of the Company of
> Jesus or a Jesuit, and that I came over in order to
> convert my country and to invite sinners to repent-
> ance. All this I will never deny; this is the duty of
> my calling. If you find anything else in me that is
> not agreeable to my profession, show me no favor.
> Meantime, act according to your conscience and re-
> member you must give an account to God."

As a poet Henry Walpole was not in the same class
as Robert Southwell, but in his prose we can surely
hear the authentic note of his hero, Edmund Campion.

On April 7, 1595, Henry Walpole was dragged to
York's public execution ground, the Knavesmire,
where he suffered the death which Edmund had

undergone more than 14 years before. His head was stuck on a pike on Micklegate Bar.

In England's Public Record Office is a document, bearing what purports to be Henry Walpole's signature. It renounces the Pope's authority, promises never to return to popery, accepts the queen's spiritual authority, and promises to preach in support of it.

Yet the signature is written in a firm, clear hand, and we know from Father Gerard that after the torture Henry could scarcely write at all. And if the document is indeed genuine, why was it never mentioned at his trial, his execution, or at any time before or afterwards?

9
South of the River

For weeks the pursuivants had been watching the house of Jane Wiseman, a Catholic widow in Essex whose husband had left her with a comfortable income and whose devotion to the old faith was well known. The comings and goings convinced them that the house was indeed being used to shelter priests and that it was almost certainly a Mass center as well.

When they raided it, however, they found only Jane and her servants at home. Chagrined, they arrested her on suspicion and bore her off to London's Gatehouse prison.

They needed more evidence, they knew that well enough. What they had would never secure a conviction, especially if Jane came before a judge who was soft on women or, worse still, on papists.

While they muttered and scratched their heads, Jane serenely occupied her time with reading and with prayer. As a lady of means she could have employed a maid to look after her. Instead, she chose to do her own cooking and washing, sending the money so saved to the poor.

Since the evidence against her was not strong enough, Jane must be framed. Easy for her captors to decide this, not so easy to accomplish it. To manufacture evidence was going to be much more difficult now that Jane was in custody and the priests keeping away from her home.

It was Nicholas Blackwell, a hanger-on of Topcliffe's, who came up with what seemed a really smart solution. For weeks Blackwell, in his role as undercover agent, had been watching a Welshman named John Buckley—real name John Jones—whom he correctly suspected of being a priest. He and John had become, indeed, quite friendly.

"The ulcer on your leg, Master Buckley, it is better, I hope?" inquired Blackwell when they met apparently by chance.

"I wish I could say so," replied John ruefully, "but in truth it pains me more than ever."

"Why then, I have the very remedy for you," Nicholas told him eagerly. "Mrs. Wiseman, a poor widow now a prisoner in the Gatehouse, makes the most excellent poultices for the poor. If I spoke to her I am sure that she would be glad to apply her skill to your leg."

John pricked up his ears eagerly. He knew Jane and would be glad to have a chance to visit her. Since Blackwell had suggested it and Blackwell was a Protestant in good standing, he could now go into the jail without suspicion.

Of course it was a trap. No sooner was the poultice firmly on John's leg than Margaret was formally charged with "receiving, comforting, helping, and maintaining priests." Her simple act of kindness was sufficient to make her guilty in law.

Like Margaret Clitherow before her, Jane refused to plead. She, too, resolved that she would not let her death lie on the conscience of the jury. She received the same terrible sentence, but this time it was not carried out. Queen Elizabeth, rebuking the judges for their cruelty, ordered a reprieve.

It was John, her patient, who was destined for martyrdom. Born at Clynog Fawr, in Caernarvonshire, he was apparently a secular priest before becoming a Franciscan. During this period of his life we find him a prisoner at Wisbech Castle; how and why he was released we are not told.

He succeeded in reaching Rome and it was there that he became a Franciscan. In 1592, at his own request, his superiors sent him to England.

Arriving in London, he stayed for a time at the house of Father John Gerard, that remarkable Jesuit whom we have already met briefly and whom we will meet again later. For four years the Welshman ministered in the capital until, soon after his visit to Jane Wiseman, Topcliffe had him arrested. The next two years he spent in the Clink prison, where he did much good work for the large number of Catholics who came to visit him.

His trial opened on July 23, 1598. In order to save 12 simple men from being implicated in his judicial murder, he refused to be tried by a jury.

"It is sufficiently clear that you have never contrived anything against the queen," Judge Clinche admitted, "but you are a priest of the Roman Church and have come here against the laws, and this constitutes treason."

"If this be a crime I own myself guilty," John replied, "for I am a priest and came over into England to gain as many souls as I could to Christ."

Condemned to death, he fell on his knees and thanked God in a loud voice.

John Jones was executed, not at Tyburn, but at a

spot south of the River Thames which used to be called St. Thomas's Watering, because here pilgrims bound for Canterbury made the first stop to water their horses. It stands at the junction of Albany Road and the Old Kent Road—a place not much visited by tourists, though known to Chaucer lovers as the point at which his pilgrims began to tell their Canterbury tales.

When John was dragged there on July 12, a bizarre mistake delayed his execution. The hangman forgot to bring the rope.

During the hour's wait until the rope was fetched John prayed and talked to the crowd. Though condemned for treason, he protested once more that he was a loyal subject.

"I have never spoken a word or entertained a thought in my whole life against the queen or my country," he declared, "but have prayed daily for their welfare."

Whether because the crowd was on his side, or because the hangman wanted to atone for forgetting the rope, John was allowed to hang until he was dead. His head, set up on a pike in Southwark, retained its natural color for two days, after which officers took it down to disfigure it and blacken it with powder.

Two years later another martyr died on this same spot in South London; not a priest, this time, but a layman named John Rigby who almost certainly knew John Jones and was possibly reconciled to the Church by him.

Like Margaret Ward young John Rigby came from a genteel family in the northwest of England and like her he was compelled, because his family had fallen on hard times, to go south and seek work as a servant. Though we have no actual evidence, it is quite likely that both families were impoverished by the fines inflicted on recusants—Catholics who refused to attend the Anglican church.

His first employers were Protestants and John, who came from the Catholic county of Lancashire, found himself pressed to worship with them. To his bitter regret, he obeyed.

Unable to live with his conscience, he went to confession. According to his own statement after his arrest, it was John Jones who reconciled him during a visit which the young Lancastrian paid to him in the Clink prison. However, it may well have been the Jesuit Father John Gerard who absolved him. In his own autobiography Father Gerard says John Rigby gave the Welsh martyr's name because he was safely dead, whereas the Jesuit was very much alive. If that is so, the answer clearly implied some kind of mental reservation.

Reconciled John certainly was, and to remove himself from any further temptation he found a new job with a Catholic family called Huddlestone who lived at Sawston Hall, near Cambridge. (To this day the house, with its priest's hiding hole, still stands and the Huddlestones still live there.)

When the daughter of his new employer, a Mrs. Fortescue, was summoned for failing to attend Anglican worship, John was sent to London to explain to the court that she was too ill to appear. Sir Richard Martin, one of the commissioners, began to question John about his own religion. John answered point-blank that he was a Catholic and that he refused to acknowledge the queen's religious supremacy.

Locked up for the night in Newgate jail, he was brought before the Lord Chief Justice on the following day. Not long ago he had been so afraid of displeasing his Protestant master that he had apostatized. Now he stood up boldly to England's senior judge. What happened next John tells us in his own words, written in prison:

> "Then my lord commanded the keeper to take me and to put on me an iron chain, which, when it came, I willed him to put it on in God's name, and said aloud, I would not change my chain for my Lord Mayor's great chain; and I gave the fellow sixpence for his pains. By and by my Lord Chief Justice sent me word to provide (prepare) myself, for I was to be arraigned forthwith. I bid the messenger tell his lordship, I never heard so good news in my life before."

At the opening of the trial one of the judges, Gaudy, asked if it were true, as reported, that John had now decided to be sensible and attend Anglican worship. John replied indignantly that it was not true and that whoever had said it of him was no friend of his.

"We see now thou art a resolute, wilful fellow and there is no remedy, but law must proceed," declared one of Gaudy's colleagues.

"Let me have law in the name of Jesus; God's will be done," John replied.

Nevertheless, Gaudy was determined that John should not die if he could help it. He strove to save him, just as Clench had striven for the life of Margaret Clitherow.

"If you will say here, before the jury, that you will go to church, we will proceed no further," he said, when John appeared again next day.

"My lord," John replied, "I would not wish you to think I have—as I hope—risen this many steps towards heaven, only to let my foot slip and fall into the bottomless pit of hell. I hope in Jesus. He will strengthen me to suffer a thousand deaths, if I had so many lives to lose."

When the jury was asked for its verdict, the foreman, ashamed and upset, mumbled inaudibly.

"Speak up, man, and be not afraid!" John encouraged him cheerfully.

Before pronouncing sentence, Gaudy tried once more.

"Good Rigby," he said, "think not I desire your death. Will you go to church?"

"No, my lord."

After the sentence was pronounced, John told the judge, "That is a fleabite in comparison of what it pleased my sweet savior Jesus to suffer for my salvation. I freely forgive your lordship and the poor jury, and all other persecutors whatever."

Gaudy obtained a three-month stay of execution in the hope that John might yet change his mind. When he appeared in court once more, the shackles fell from his legs. The jailer riveted them on more tightly than ever, but again they fell off. Many of those present were sure that they had witnessed a miracle.

On June 21, 1600, John Rigby was told that he was to die that day. *"Deo Gratias,"* he replied. "It is the best tidings that ever were brought me since the day I was born."

As he was dragged to the scaffold the earl of Rutland and a certain Captian Whitlock saw the procession and stopped it to ask the man on the hurdle who he was and why he was to die. When John told them about himself, Captain Whitlock tried, as Gaudy had done, to persuade him to conform. Seeing that he could not succeed, the captain declared, "Then I see thou hast worthily deserved a virgin's crown; I pray God send thee the kingdom of heaven; I desire thee pray for me."

When the hangman helped him into the cart John

gave him a gold piece as a token of his forgiveness. He kissed the rope as it was put about his neck and began to address the crowd. The sheriff, interrupting, urged him to pray for the queen. John did so, very affectionately.

Despite the good impression which he had made, John Rigby was executed with great cruelty. Cut down while still conscious, he cried out as the butchers began their work, "God forgive you, Jesus receive my soul."

At this point a common porter, who was standing by, put his foot on John's throat so that he could say no more. When he died he was 30 years old.

The earl and the captain had ridden behind to witness the execution. Captain Whitlock, at least, never forgot the man whose life he had tried to save. Often, in the years to come, he told the story of John Rigby's death, observing that he had never known anyone show such modesty, patience and resolution in his religion.

10
The Housekeeper

It stood on the corner of St. Clement's Lane: a large, rickety house whose gables lurched precariously over the street; a plain, honest looking house with nothing secretive about it. No one hunting popish priests would expect to find them here.

Yet this was, in the dying years of the 16th century, the hub of the Catholic mission in London. Here, in disguise, came young Jesuits from the continent, eager to follow in the footsteps of Edmund Campion and Henry Walpole. Here, too, secular priests found a welcome, and the Franciscan John Jones. For many, St. Clement's Lane was the first stop on the road to martyrdom.

The hearty, sporting gentleman who owned the house we have already briefly met. Father John Gerard, a Lancashire-born Jesuit, combined deep holiness with the panache of a courtier, the iron nerve of a secret agent, and the drive of a business tycoon. He moved around London with a self-assurance which few of his colleagues equalled, making friends in-

stantly with people who would have been horrified to
know his true identity. His autobiography, telling the
story of his capture, torture, and escape from the
Tower, compares for sheer excitement with any adventure yarn.

Though he risked death constantly, John Gerard did
not die a martyr. Recalled to Belgium, he ended his
days peacefully in bed. The story we have to tell is
that of the lady who kept house for him, who must
often have opened the door to the young priests newly
arrived in England. Her name was Anne Line.

Born at Dunmow, Essex, Anne was the daughter of a
Calvinist father who disowned and disinherited her
when she was received into the Catholic Church. Her
brother also became a Catholic and suffered the same
fate.

At the age of 19 she married Roger Line, a convert
like herself, who was arrested soon afterwards for
attending Mass. Exiled to Flanders, he died there in
1594, leaving Anne without any means of support.

Jane Wiseman, who herself came so near to martyrdom, gave Anne shelter in her home for a while. When
John Gerard asked her to take charge of his reception
center for priests, he did not need to spell out the
dangers. Anne accepted the job without hesitation.

From the very outset Anne Line wanted to be a
martyr. As we have seen, that was not true of John
Houghton or of Edmund Campion, each of whom at
first hoped for a peaceable solution to his dilemma.
It was not true of Thomas More, who used all his
lawyer's skill in his efforts to stay alive. Though these
great saints gladly gave their lives when they saw that
it was what God wanted of them, they did not seek
martyrdom as their foremost ambition. With Anne
Line it was different. She deeply envied the priests
whom she received at the house in St. Clement's

Lane. Soon, perhaps within weeks, they would have the privilege of dying for their faith. But what chance had she, a poor Martha, of earning a martyr's crown?

Caring constantly for priests who were risking their lives, she does not seem to have realized that she was herself exposed to the danger of torture and death. In any case, her health was not good; she suffered from severe headaches and from dropsy, and knew that in the insalubrious air of the capital she could hardly expect to live to a ripe old age.

Her great hope lay in a promise given to her by her confessor, Father William Thomson, seven years before. If he himself were found worthy to die for the faith, he had said, he would pray for her in heaven that she might receive the same privilege.

Father Thomson was executed at Tyburn on April 20, 1586. From what followed, we may fairly assume that he did not forget his promise to Anne.

After she had once helped him to escape from the pursuivants, keeping them talking while he made his exit, she eventually saw him captured and had to leave the house in St. Clement's Lane. Moving into a house of her own, she regularly entertained priests there and invited Catholic friends for Mass.

On Candlemas Day, 1601, the celebrant was the Jesuit Father Francis Page. Anne had gathered a larger congregation than she would ever have risked during her days with Father Gerard.

The neighbors alerted the authorities, and in no time the house was raided. Though Father Page had managed to hide his vestments, the room was full of people and the altar prepared for Mass.

Looking around them, the men demanded to know whether there was a priest present.

"We are waiting for the priest to come," said one of the guests equivocally.

Experienced at their task, the men stared around them. Father Page was in lay dress, but they knew instinctively that this was their man; his tranquil and modest look had betrayed him.

The more spirited members of the congregation started to argue that they were awaiting the priest and in the commotion that followed somebody opened the door of the room. There was nothing tranquil about Father Page now. Shaking himself free of his captors, he darted out and was in the secret hiding place before the priest catchers properly realized what had happened.

Though they turned the house upside down they did not find the priest—but they had Anne.

At her trial she was so weak that she had to be carried into court in a chair. The evidence against her was scarcely impressive. It consisted of one witness, a man named Marriott who deposed that he had seen a man dressed in white in her house.

For Chief Justice Popham, an anti-Catholic fanatic, this was enough. He directed the jury to bring in a verdict of guilty. For Anne the sentence held no terror; as she read her prayers in prison on the previous day, a light had shone around her book.

On February 27, 1601, Anne Line was taken to Tyburn with Father Roger Filcock, her Jesuit confessor, and the Benedictine Father Mark Barkworth. At the scaffold she found the usual Protestant ministers waiting to persuade her to abandon her Catholic errors.

"Away with you," she told them bluntly. "I have nothing in common with any of you."

To the crowd she called out loudly, "I am sentenced to die for harboring a Catholic priest, and so far am I from repenting for having done so that I wish, with all my soul, that where I have entertained one, I could have entertained a thousand."

She then knelt to pray, and continued praying until the hangman had finished his work.

In her will Anne bequeathed her bed to Father Gerard. He never received it, but he did get hold of the coverlet. Ever afterwards, when he was in London, he slept under it and felt safer in consequence.

Father Page's freedom lasted only until the following year. Brought up a Protestant, this young man had become a convert after falling in love with a Catholic girl. In the end he did not marry her but became a priest instead.

After his escape from Anne's house he continued in his ministry in the capital, only to be betrayed by a young Catholic woman who had sold her soul to the priest catchers. As he went out one night she spotted him in the street and hurried after him calling out, "Mr. Page, I want to speak to you!"

Unable to shake her off, Francis dived into the nearest house and asked the owner to let him out by the back door. The girl, meanwhile, cried out that there was a priest and a traitor inside, and a crowd gathered. The people inside the house refused to let Francis go and he was swiftly arrested. He faced death at Tyburn with the joy which Anne and so many other martyrs had shown there.

11
Little John

Nobody took much notice of the little workman as he went about his tasks. A new gate for the pigsty, some missing slates replaced on the kitchen roof—there were always repairs to be done on a big, rambling house like Braddocks. Soon the workman became a familiar sight to the tradesmen and other regular visitors. Efficient and self-effacing, he never spoke unless spoken to first, and then he replied as briefly as possible. Asked his name, he would smile. "They call me Little John," he would reply—and turn back to his work.

Braddocks was the Essex home of Jane Wiseman, the widow whom we met during her imprisonment in the Gatehouse. In the first floor of the house Jane had a chapel, and when hammer blows and the sound of bricks being moved rang through the building, it caused no surprise. Just Little John making a few alterations upstairs.

But now the little man was working with a new intensity, for this was the biggest job of all and it had to be done quickly. It he were overlong people might start to ask questions or gossip in the village, or perhaps some overcurious intruder might stumble in and discover him at his task.

The prying stranger would have been astonished to discover that John, having removed the tiles from the fireplace, had burrowed down into the solid brickwork beneath it. Below lay a large living room which also had its own fireplace. At a point just above and to the right of this, he hollowed out a space big enough for a man to hide in. Only lath and plaster, and the panelled wainscot, separated it from the living room itself.

It was beautifully done and cunningly disguised. In the chapel the workman had constructed a false hearth so convincing in its appearance that nobody would have suspected that it was really the escape route to a secret chamber below.

But who was Little John?

His real name was Nicholas Owen and he was a Jesuit lay brother, though so silent was he that even some of his fellow Jesuits were never sure whether or not he belonged to the Society. An Oxfordshire man, Nicholas was the genius who built and designed many of the hiding holes in great Catholic homes up and down England: places where hunted priests frequently hid undiscovered for days while the priest catchers ripped the house apart around them.

His strategy was always the same. First he would do some straightforward repairs in order to make those who were not "in the know" familiar with his presence. Once accepted as part of the household, he could set about his real work.

Today that work can still be seen at Braddocks (now a farmhouse); at Sawston Hall, the Cambridgeshire house where John Rigby found work; at Hinlip Hall in Worcestershire; and at Harrowden in Northamptonshire.

In other houses also, now destroyed, Nicholas exercised his skill. For 25 years he moved around England, often carrying out the most secret part of the operation by night, moving the stones and brickwork with his bare hands despite his slender physique.

Little John was Nicholas Owen. But who was Nicholas Owen?

Even though his life has been examined by the rigorous processes of canonization and even though he has left us tangible evidence of his skill and devotion, Nicholas remains a shadowy figure. Had he lived in the 20th century, he might have provided a spy fiction writer—John Le Carré, perhaps—with an excellent model.

About his early training as a builder and joiner we know next to nothing, but he was certainly a trained craftsman when, in 1580 or shortly before, he entered the Society of Jesus. He was not only the builder of the hiding holes but also their architect. Even today his ingenuity makes experts marvel.

We do know that before beginning work on a new hiding hole, Nicholas always received Holy Communion. Each project was a fresh test of his skill, for each had to be unique: the discovery of one hiding place must give no clue to the location of those elsewhere. Wherever possible, as at Braddocks, he bored down into solid brick or stonework, so that the cavity would give no tell-tale hollow sound. He nearly always managed to fit a bolt hole into his designs—an emergency exit through which the priest could wriggle if the searchers got too close to the principal entrance. He was also fond of building one hiding place within another, and sometimes a third one within that, so that if the first were discovered the searchers might think it empty and look no further.

His skill must have won the heartfelt admiration, above all, of the priests whose lives it saved. Yet

Nicholas was, we may feel sure, a difficult man to compliment. Even when alone with fellow Jesuits, he never entered into the sort of friendly banter which would have shown them that he was indeed one of their number. Instead he always spoke, when he spoke at all, exactly as though he were a servant, and the priests whom he served—Edmund Campion and John Gerard among them—respected his desire for self-effacement.

It seems ironical that on one of the few occasions when he did speak out boldly, his forthrightness should have landed him in jail. It happened after Edmund Campion's execution, when Nicholas proclaimed the martyr's innocence so loudly that he was arrested and thrown into the prison known as the Counter. His captors did not know that he was the architect of the hiding holes, but they tortured him in an effort to make him reveal the whereabouts of priest. Having got nothing out of him, they released him in return for money paid by a Catholic gentleman.

When a horse shied and crushed his foot Nicholas was badly hurt and slightly crippled, but the disability did not hinder his work. Betrayed by a servant of Jane Wiseman, both he and John Gerard were arrested. Nicholas found himself once more in the Counter and was once more bailed out.

Father Gerard, however, was held in the Tower, where he had stood up bravely to the inevitable torture. By bribing a jailor, he and a companion got on to a roof from where they planned to throw an iron ball to friends waiting below. The friends would tie a rope to the ball and throw it back to the escapers so that they could lower themselves to freedom.

The first attempt failed when the boat carrying the would-be rescuers capsized in the Thames and they narrowly escaped drowning. On the next night they tried again, and succeeded. Both men got clear away from the great fortress, and John Gerard found Nicholas, who had played a major part in planning the escape, waiting with horses to carry him to safety.

The little lay brother's next assignment was as servant to Father Henry Garnet, the Jesuit provincial. In November, 1605, the so-called Gunpowder Plot sent a wave of anti-Catholic feeling through England. Many historians now suspect that the government engineered the plot in order to discredit Catholics in general and Jesuits in particular, but in the aftermath Father Garnet and Nicholas were forced to lie low at Hinlip Hall, the Worcestershire house already mentioned and the home of a Catholic named Mr. Abington. Hiding there with them was another Jesuit priest, Father Edward Oldcorne, and a lay brother, Ralph Ashley.

Suddenly the fugitives found themselves betrayed. A local justice of the peace, Henry Bromley, descended on the house with a hundred men behind him.

For six days the searchers banged and tore their way through the house, while the two priests hid in the hiding hole which Nicholas had built so skilfully years before. Starved, breathing foul air, their cramped legs swollen, they resolved to die where they were rather than betray the friends who had sheltered them.

Starvation eventually drove Nicholas and Ralph Ashley from the separate recess where they were hidden, for they had taken cover with only an apple to eat between them. Their hope was that Bromley and his men would mistake them for the priests and call off the hunt. The pursuers were not deceived, however, and went on searching for five days more, until at last they broke through to the secret chamber where the provincial and his colleague still crouched.

Edward Oldcorne and Ralph Ashley were hanged at Worcester, Henry Garnet at St. Paul's Churchyard in London. In the Tower Nicholas Owen was tortured daily for six days, for now the persecutors knew that here was the architect of the hiding holes and they were determined to drag the details of each one from him. On the rack the only words he uttered were "Jesus" and "Mary."

He was already suffering from a hernia and the torture made it worse. Afraid that he would die before he talked, the torturers fastened an iron girdle on him and hung him up for six hours at a time by iron bracelets fastened to his wrists. To increase the suffering they added weights to his feet.

He remained silent until his bowels burst open, the iron girdle tearing the wound and making it worse. And so Nicholas died, in terrible agony but with his secrets still locked within him.

Of the humble lay brother John Gerard wrote, "I verily think no man can be said to have done more good of all those who labored in the English vineyard."

12
After Guy Fawkes

Catholic priests were notoriously stubborn, but David Cecil was convinced that he would make this one talk.

"I advise you to tell me of your treasons," he threatened, "or else I will take care to draw out a confession from your mouth at your fingers' ends."

Cecil, otherwise known as Lord Burghley, was a shrewd enough character; if he were not so he would scarcely have become the monarch's right-hand man. Now, however, he was wasting his time. Thomas Garnet could not confess any treasons because he had none to confess.

Determined to have one last try, Cecil produced a letter, apparently written by Thomas's uncle Henry, implicating him in the Gunpowder Plot. Thomas immediately dismissed the letter as a forgery and Cecil could see that he was telling the truth. Galled, he had to admit that he had no shred of evidence against this priest who, in any case, feared neither rack nor thumbscrew.

For six years Thomas had worked in England as a secular priest, but shortly before his arrest he had asked his uncle to receive him into the Society of Jesus. Released from prison and banished, he made his way to Louvain, in Belgium, and became a Jesuit novice.

A year later he was back in England, stationed in Warwickshire. The Catholics of Cornwall asked if he might be sent to them, but while he was journeying westward an apostate priest named Rouse betrayed his identity.

Pressed to take the new Oath of Supremacy, he refused on the ground that it was a denial of the supremacy of the Holy See. Instead he asked to swear an oath of his own composition which ran like this: "I, Thomas Garnet, sincerely heartily profess that I will pay to my rightful King James all fidelity and obedience due to him by the law of nature and the divine law of the true Church of Christ."

The court refused to let him even finish reading this and tore the paper from his hands. So far he had refused to admit or deny that he was a priest, but now three witnesses swore that he had indeed signed himself "Thomas Garnet, priest." On their evidence he was condemned to death.

Thomas looked forward eagerly to his martyr's crown. When friends offered him an escape plan, he turned it down. He preferred, he said, to listen to an inner voice which told him, *"Noli fugere."* (Don't run away).

His face was even happier when, on June 23, 1608, he laid himself upon the hurdle and was dragged to Tyburn to be executed before a crowd which was a thousand strong. The earl of Exeter, in a last minute effort to save his life, begged him again to take the Oath of Supremacy, pointing out that several other priests had already done so and that others looked upon it as a disputable matter in which faith was not compromised. Thomas would have none of this.

"My lord," he replied, "if the case be so doubtful and disputable, how can I in conscience swear to what is doubtful as if it were certain? No, I will not take the oath, though I might have a thousand lives."

Standing in the cart, he forgave his persecutors by name: "May God pardon Rouse who betrayed me, Cross who apprehended me, the Bishop of London who thrust me into prison, Sir William Wade, the prefect of the Tower, who eagerly solicited my death and the attorney general who invented so many things against me. May all attain salvation and with me reach heaven."

He then recited the Our Father, the Hail Mary and the Apostles' Creed, and began to sing the hymn *Veni Creator*. As he did so, the cart was drawn away and, at the insistence of the earl and the crowd, Thomas was allowed to hang until he was dead.

The big roundup of November 5, 1605, included a raid on the office of a Mr. Knight, who carried on business in London's Holborn as a scrivener, a copier of legal documents. There they arrested a Welshman whose face and manner showed him to be a man of breeding. His name was John Roberts, a Benedictine priest.

John was now accused, along with Thomas Garnet and many others, of complicity in the Gunpowder Plot. Of course nothing could be proved against him and, after eight months in the Gatehouse prison, he was released at the intervention of the French ambassador.

John was of noble blood on both sides of the family, a descendant of the princely house of Llywelyn. Born at Dolgelly, he was brought up nominally as a Protestant, but his tutor was an elderly Catholic priest and John himself said that he was always a Catholic at heart.

He enrolled at St. John's College, Oxford, but before taking his degree he switched to the study of law in London. He did not stay there long either, for in the very same year, 1598, he set off on a foreign trip with the sole intention of having a good time.

The picture that emerges so far shows John as a somewhat unsettled and even frivolous young man. It is far more likely that he was seeking, perhaps unconsciously, his true calling in life. In any case, he quickly found it. At Paris, in the Cathedral of Notre Dame, John Roberts was formally reconciled to the Catholic Church. He at once set out for Spain and the English College at Valladolid.

His intention was to become a secular priest working in England; it was to train men for the home mission that the college existed. However, the town of Valladolid also contained the Benedictine monastery of San Benito, and when no fewer than eight English and Welsh students announced their intention to become monks there was strong opposition from the college's Jesuit authorities. As Benedictines, the Jesuits pointed out, they would be expected to remain in their Spanish cloister instead of returning to their homeland.

Not long before, a young man from Lincolnshire named Mark Barkworth had also wanted to become a Benedictine—the first Valladolid student to seek the habit. On February 27, 1601, Father Mark Barkworth was executed at Tyburn wearing that habit, even though he had never lived in a monastery or, apparently, ever been formally professed. The Benedictines joyfully claimed the young martyr as their own.

By now John and his companions had won their fight to enter the cloister. Inspired by Mark's example, they petitioned Pope Clement VIII for permission to work in England as monks once they were ordained. In December, 1602, the Pope granted a general permission to English and Welsh Benedictines, present and future. Three weeks later Father John Roberts was on his way.

Travelling with him was a fellow Benedictine, Father Augustine Bradshaw. It took them three months to reach London, where they arrived disguised in plumed hats, doublets, and swords. This unmonastic costume did not deceive the authorities, and the pair were swiftly arrested and deported.

Within weeks John was back in London. During an epidemic, so severe that it killed off 30,000 people in the first year, he worked heroically and made many converts. Of him a contemporary wrote, "Amid all the Religious who have worked in that island this man may almost be reckoned as the chief, both as regards labor and fruitfulness of preaching." Other writers also praise him highly.

Like all missionaries of the time, John was in constant danger from spies. His particular enemy was another Welshman living in London, Lewis Owen. Strangely, it was this embittered Protestant who drew a comparison between John and an earlier monk-missionary. "Roberts," he wrote dryly, "was the first that had his mission from the Pope and his own Spanish prelate to go for England, which made him not a little proud that he should be a second Augustine monk, to convert and reconcile his countrymen to the Roman antichrist."

In the spring of 1604, John travelled to the south coast with four young postulants, bound for a general chapter of his Benedictine congregation. Once more he was arrested, but this time his captors failed to identify him as a priest and he was released. Then came the Gunpowder Plot, the arrest in Holborn, and his eventual deportation for the second time.

This time he stayed abroad for more than a year, during which time he and Augustine Bradshaw played a major part in founding a monastery for the English and Welsh monks at Douai. Today this flourishes in Somerset as the famous Abbey of Downside.

The year 1607 found John back in England. Arrested yet again, he refused to take the revised Oath of Supremacy and managed to escape from the Gatehouse prison. He stayed free until 1609, when he once more found himself behind bars and was rescued a second time by the French ambassador.

Hearing that the plague had once again broken out in London, he returned from Douai to be with his stricken flock. By now he must have known that authority's patience was running out and that if he did not die from disease he would almost certainly face the hangman's rope.

Arrested on the first Sunday of Advent just as he reached the end of Mass, he was brought before Edward Coke, who had prosecuted Robert Southwell and was now Lord Chief Justice of England. Beside him sat George Abbot, the Bishop of London.

With John in the dock was Thomas Somers, a secular priest from Westmorland. After both men had refused the oath, John admitted that he was a priest and a monk who had come to work for the good of souls "and would continue to do were I to live longer."

When Abbot called him a disturber and seducer of the people, John replied boldly that if he was, then so was St. Augustine, for he had been sent to England by the same Apostolic See. Ordered to be silent, he attacked Protestant errors and rebuked Abbot for sitting in a secular court on a capital charge. He appealed to the judges to decide the case themselves and not to let the deaths of Thomas and himself rest on the consciences of simple jurymen. The request was ignored, the jury did what their betters expected of them, and the two priests were condemned to hang at Tyburn.

On the night before the execution, a Spanish lady named Luisa de Carvajal bribed the Newgate jailer to transfer John and Thomas to the company of other Catholic prisoners. There they held a remarkable party, Dona Luisa at the head of the table and the condemned priests on either side of her. Around them sat 18 other guests, all in prison for their faith.

So jolly was the mood that John began to worry that his high spirits might seem disedifying.

"Had I not better withdraw and give myself to prayer?" he asked his hostess.

"No, certainly not," she replied. "You cannot be better employed than by letting them see with what cheerful courage you are about to die for Christ."

Before the party broke up Luisa washed the feet of the two martyrs, which greatly angered King James I when he heard about it.

At Tyburn they found 16 common felons who were also to be hanged that day. One of the officers, apparently sympathetic, pointed out to John that he was to die alongside thieves, like the master whom he served. However, when John invited the criminals to confess their belief in the Catholic Church and receive absolution, he was quickly cut short.

Led to the cart, John jokingly offered to leap into it. Weak from an illness, he had to be helped. A kindly sheriff gave him a glass of brandy and he drank a little. Somebody advised him to put on his nightcap.

"Do you think I fear the headache?" he asked with a smile.

During his last speech to the crowd he was interrupted by the same officer who had tried to prevent him from reconciling the felons. Another officer took John's part, insisting that he was saying nothing against king or State. He was allowed to finish.

Before the cart was driven away the two priests embraced and gave each other a final blessing. Both were dead when the final butchery began.

13
Three Lancashire Men

It was a brilliant performance—one of the best ever seen in the Roman College. For hours the young man had stood before an audience of leading academics, defending a host of theses from every branch of theology. Every question was answered, every objection met. Not once did John Almond falter in his replies.

Had he chosen to remain in Rome, John would certainly have been a huge success as a professor, but that life was not for him. Everyone present in the great hall knew that this gifted young scholar would soon die a martyr's death. Moved by the thought, the Oratorian Cardinal Baronius, who was presiding, kissed his head reverently while the applause echoed round them in waves.

John was born at Allerton, then a country village, but now a suburb of Liverpool. While still a boy he went to live in Ireland, until he sailed off to Douai to begin his studies for the priesthood. Later he transferred to Rome's English College.

Of his ten years on the English mission we unfortunately know very little, though we may be sure that he had his share of dangers and hairs-breadth escapes. We have one contemporary description, obviously written by someone who knew him well. Though it still used the stilted language then thought appropriate, it does tell us something about the man himself.

John was, says this author, "a reprover of sin, a good example to follow; of an ingenious and acute understanding, sharp and apprehensive in his conceits and answers, yet complete with modesty, full of courage, and ready to suffer for Christ that suffered for him. Of his stature, neither high nor low, but indifferent; a body lean, either by nature or through ghostly discipline; a face lean, his head blackish brown; in his conversation mild, learned and persuasive, and worthy to be remembered of those that did converse with him."

His success as a missionary made him a marked man. Spies were set to trap him, and in March, 1612, he was arrested, loaded with chains, and thrown into a dark underground cell in Newgate. There he spent 24 hours without food and drink, and with only the damp ground to lie on. During this ordeal Protestant ministers came to dispute with him. Needless to say, they proved no match for him and were quickly reduced to silence.

Of his examination before the Bishop of London, John himself afterwards wrote an account. The bishop, John King, was newly appointed and perhaps out to make an impression on the audience. If so, his attempt to get a rise out of his victim only made King himself look foolish.

King: What countryman are you?

John: A Lancashire man.

King: In what place were you born?

John: About Allerton.

King: About Allerton! Mark the equivocation; then not in Allerton?

John: No equivocation; I was not born in Allerton, but in the edge or side of Allerton.

King: You were born under a hedge then, were you?

John: Many a better man than I, or you either, has been born under a hedge.

King: What, you cannot remember that you were born in a house?

John: Can you?

King: My mother told me so.

John: Then you remember not that you were born in a house, but only that your mother told you so; so much I remember too.

Having failed to unsettle John with his buffoonery, King now gets down to the serious business of trying to make him admit that he is a priest. John cleverly uses Protestant doctrine to parry the questions.

King: Were you ever beyond the seas?

John: I have been to Ireland.

King: How long since you came thence?

John: I remember not how long since, neither is it material.

King: Here is plain answering, is it not?

John: More plain than you would give, if you were examined by some of ours in another place.

King: I ask, are you a priest?

John: I am not Christ; and unless I were Christ, in your own grounds, *yours* I mean, I cannot be a priest.

King: Though you cannot be one in our grounds, are you one in your own?

John: If I be none, nor can be any in your grounds, which allow no other priesthood, nor other priest but Christ, and you are bound to maintain your own grounds, and uphold the truth of them, you might well forbear this question, and suppose for certain that I am no priest.

King: Are you a priest, yea or no?

John: No man accuseth me.

King: Then, this is all the answer I shall have?

John: All I can give unless proof come in.

King: Where have you lived, and where have you spent your time?

John: Here is an orderly course of justice, sure! What is it material where I have lived, or how I have spent my time, all the while I am accused of no evils?

John's verbal pyrotechnics could not save him, as he well knew, for he had to refuse the Oath of Supremacy. At Tyburn he scattered money to the crowd and gave the executioner a gold piece, making it clear that the gift was not intended to procure any gentle treatment on the gallows.

Forty-five years old, John was prematurely aged and his hair was now grey, yet he did not shiver in the cold morning air. Was it a good custom, he asked the crowd, to blindfold his eyes before he died? The crowd replied that it was, and a handkerchief was quickly handed to him.

When the cart was driven away, bystanders jumped forward to swing on his legs and so shorten his suffering, as they had done for John Payne at Chelmsford 30 years before.

After John's death the waggish Bishop of London fell into a deep depression from which he never recovered. Apparently, John Almond had made a deep impression upon him and the execution preyed on his mind. According to some reports, King eventually became a Catholic and prayed devoutly to the man whom he had condemned. If that is true, perhaps he was at last able to smile again.

Not many miles from John Almond's Liverpool birthplace lies the town of Haydock. Today it is famous for its racecourse, but in the 16th century it was the home of the Arrowsmiths, a family who, like many another in Lancashire, doggedly clung to the old faith through generations of persecution.

The little boy born to Robert and Margery Arrowsmith in 1585 was christened Brian. At Confirmation, however, he chose the name Edmund, and it is as Edmund Arrowsmith that he is remembered today.

As soon as he was old enough to understand, the youngster must have been told of his grandfather, Thurstan Arrowsmith, who lost his property and died in jail rather than give up his religion. He must also have chortled with delight at the story of his maternal grandfather, Nicholas Gerard, who was forcibly carried to the Anglican service when suffering from gout. Placed up against the pulpit, he sang psalms in Latin so loudly that his tormentors were forced to carry him out again. (The Welsh martyr Richard Gwyn, you may recall, reacted to the same treatment in similar style.)

It was not long before little Brian got his first taste of persecution. He was not much than a baby when the pursuivants, eager to catch a priest, burst into the Arrowsmith homestead and thrust their swords into every hole, every bed, every conceivable hiding place. Finding nothing, they took the parents off to jail and left their four tiny children, whom they had dragged from their beds, shivering in their night clothes until neighbors came to look after them.

After bribing his way out of jail, Robert Arrowsmith took the pressure off his wife and children by going abroad with his brother to fight as a soldier in the Low Countries. They never saw him again, for he died from his wounds in Brussels.

Looking down from heaven, Robert must have been

proud of his children, and of Brian especially. Each
morning, as they walked to school, they all recited part
of the Little Office of Our Lady. Each evening, when
he came home, Brian recited the Jesus Psalter and
other devotions. Yet the youngster was in no way
sanctimonious; he had a cheerful, winning personality
and even his Protestant schoolmasters were very fond
of him.

At Douai, where he became Edmund, illness interrupted his studies and he had to return to England for
a spell. Back at the college he worked so hard that
illness threatened once more. His superiors decided
that he should be ordained early and sent home for
good.

As a priest he retained all his schoolboy sense of
fun. He was not a handsome or imposing man, yet
what he lacked in appearance he made up for in
personality. After his death a fellow missioner wrote a
pen-picture:

> "Though his presence was very mean, yet he was
> both zealous, witty and fervent, and so forward in
> disputing with heretics that I often wished him mer-
> rily to carry salt in his pocket to season his actions, lest
> too much zeal without discretion might bring him too
> soon into danger, considering the vehement and sud-
> den storms of persecution that often assailed us,"

If, as sometimes happened, Edmund and his friends
met some sumptuously mounted group of Protestant
ministers, he would invariably want to start a theological argument which might easily lead to trouble.
When that happened his companions would anxiously
pull his sleeve.

On one occasion, however, it was a Protestant who
took the initiative. Misled by Edmund's "mean presence" and suspecting that he was a priest, he tried to
get a rise out of the little man. When his witty sallies
were cleverly turned back upon himself, the Protes-

tant swore a great oath. "I thought I had met with a silly fellow," he declared, "but now I see he is either a foolish scholar or a learned fool."

Interestingly, Edmund gained a considerable reputation as an exorcist, though he never attempted to cast out devils without first seeking the help of other priests. At this distance in time it is impossible to know how many of those whom he helped were truly possessed, and how many simple victims of some psychological disorder.

For ten or eleven years he worked in his native county as a secular priest. Then, in 1624, he answered a long-felt call to enter the Society of Jesus. His novitiate was short: two or three months spent on retreat in London. Then he headed back north to Lancashire.

He had already been arrested once but was soon released, along with many other Catholic prisoners, because King James I was hoping to marry his son to a Spanish princess and wanted to make a pleasing gesture in Spain's direction. On that occasion he had been hauled before the Bishop of Chester, whom he found digging into a meat dinner in the company of many other clerics. Since it was Lent the bishop was somewhat embarrassed. In the matter of fasting and abstinence, he well knew, Catholics put Anglicans to shame.

He explained that it was quite in order for him to eat meat since, being old and weak, he had received a dispensation to do so.

"Indeed?" replied Edmund dryly. "And who has dispensed your lusty ministers here, who have no such need?"

The remark can scarcely have assisted clerical digestions.

In the village of Brindle, near Preston, there stands to this day a fine Tudor dwelling known as "the house of the last Mass." Tradition has it that this is where Edmund offered the Holy Sacrifice for the last time before his second and final arrest in 1628. A renegade Catholic, whom he had rebuked for marrying his cousin before a Protestant minister, had told a local justice that the Jesuit Arrowsmith was at that very moment riding along the road to Blackburn.

A gang of ruffians followed and overtook him. Though they were armed with swords and Edmund only with a stick, the little priest fought vigorously before he was overpowered and dragged off to a local inn, the Boar's Head, which also flourishes today. Here he was locked in the cattle shed while his captors went inside for a celebratory drink.

On August 26, he was brought before Mr. Justice Yelverton at the assizes in Lancaster Castle. Humbly, he asked for a public debate, offering to defend his faith against all comers. His offer was brusquely refused.

"Then I will defend it with my life," he declared, at which the judge flew into a rage.

"I will not leave this town until I see your bowels burnt before your face," he stormed. Repeatedly, he threatened Edmund with death.

"And you too, my lord, must die," replied Edmund calmly.

During the two days which passed between sentence and execution he was locked in a dark hole, where he could not properly lie down, with heavy bolts fastened to his legs. Deprived of food and drink, he was watched constantly by three or four men, and nobody was allowed to speak to him.

Also held prisoner in Lancaster Castle that August day was John Southworth, a secular priest who was himself to be martyred and canonized. As Edmund was dragged out through the castle yard, John stretched his hands between the bars of his cell window to give him absolution.

Hoping to forestall any display of popular support, the judge had the execution carried out a day earlier than expected, at a time when most townsfolk would normally be at their midday meal. When Edmund reached the execution ground, however, he found nearly the whole town waiting to see him die. From the ladder he urged them to take care of their souls, than which nothing was more precious, and to become good Catholics.

A Protestant minister made the usual last minute offer of life if he would conform to the Anglican religion.

"Oh, sir, how far I am from that!" exclaimed Edmund. "Tempt me no more. I am a dying man. I will do it in no case, on no condition."

It was now becoming customary to spare condemned priests the worst tortures of the obscene death sentence. Hacked off after his death, Edmund's head was placed on John of Gaunt's Tower at Lancaster and his quarters were hung from the castle walls.

On Easter morning, 1641, the Rev. James Gatley, vicar of Leigh, mounted the pulpit and announced to his congregation that there was a task more important than Divine Service awaiting them. At Morleys Hall, home of a Catholic family nearby, the notorious priest Ambrose Barlow was certainly celebrating Mass at that very moment. As good Protestants, they ought to go and capture him.

Minutes later the mob was on its way, the vicar striding along in front. Four hundred people, who had gathered that day to greet the risen Christ, burst into the rambling old house where a group of terrified Catholics faced them.

"Where is Barlow?" they yelled. "He is the man we want."

A frail, bearded man stepped forward. Poorly dressed, he was full of quiet dignity.

"I am Ambrose Barlow," he said.

When the Protestants were first heard hammering at the door, some of his congregation had begged Ambrose to take cover in one of the hiding holes with which the hall was well provided. Yet Ambrose could not seek safety for himself when it meant leaving these innocent people, many of them women and children, to the mercy of their bloodthirsty enemies. England, now on the brink of civil war, was in the grip of a new and terrible anti-Catholic fever. The mob, primed with wild stories of popish plots, might easily vent their anger on the flock if the shepherd escaped.

Seizing Ambrose, they dragged him before a local magistrate who ordered him to be taken to Lancaster. The journey, more than 50 miles, was itself an ordeal for a man who had, not long before, suffered a serious stroke.

That he would be martyred here, he had no doubt. While Edmund Arrowsmith was awaiting trial Ambrose had managed to bring him the sacraments in this very same castle where he himself was now a prisoner. When Edmund was executed Ambrose was far away and on the following night still had not received the news. Suddenly, he saw Edmund standing at his bedside.

"I have suffered and now you will suffer," he said. "Say little, for they will endeavor to take hold of your words."

Like Edmund, Ambrose Barlow was born in 1585, the year in which it was made high treason for a priest to be within the queen's dominions. His family lived at Barlow Hall in Chorlton-cum-Hardy, a village now absorbed into Manchester, where Ambrose's birth-place survives as the headquarters of the local golf club.

The little boy, fourth of 14 children, was baptized Edward; he became Ambrose when, in 1614 he joined his brother William in the Benedictine Order.

Although he came from a staunchly Catholic fam-ily—his grandfather, like Edmund Arrowsmith's, had died in prison for the faith—young Edward spent part of his boyhood as a Protestant. At the age of 12 when Elizabethan persecution was at its height, he was taken from school to become a page boy in a Protestant household in Cheshire. Almost certainly this was done by order of the government, which frequently transplanted Catholic children in order to deprive them of their faith.

The efforts of a Catholic neighbor, Lady Margaret Davenport, rescued Edward from Protestantism. Soon afterwards, he followed William to Douai. Though both brothers became monks, their careers followed very different paths. William, who took the name Rudesind, remained abroad to become a distinguished canon lawyer and, eventually, the president general of the English Benedictine Congregation.

Dom Ambrose, on the other hand, returned to En-gland in 1617, almost as soon as he was ordained. Though he certainly visited his family home, it was at Morleys Hall that he made his headquarters. The Tyldesley family, who owned the house, was anxious that a priest should take care of the poor Catholics in their neighborhood and provided money for the pur-pose. It was upon this that Ambrose lived.

Though his health was never good he was con-stantly on the move, tramping miles over rough moor-land roads and often celebrating several Masses in one day. And yet, as his contemporary biographer quaintly puts it, "notwithstanding his informities I never knew him to tamper with the physicians. Surely, he was to himself Dr. Diet, Dr. Quiet and the only Dr. Merriman that I ever knew."

Quiet and yet merry, too—that seems to sum up Ambrose's personality well. He had none of Edmund Arrowsmith's dash and verve, and he did not go around picking arguments with Protestants. Yet he constantly showed courage, and he expected others to show it also. Told that certain Catholic gentry did not care to risk being seen at Mass, he observed dryly, "I like not those that will be peeping at God."

Vainglory he also disliked; often he used his dry wit as a weapon against it. He certainly had none himself and he took no pride at all in his appearance. His forked beard was left untrimmed and his clothes were old-fashioned. His neckerchief was of the poorest quality, his best hat not worth twopence, and his shoes old and scuffed. Despite the dangers which he faced, he carried no arms. "Indeed, I dare not wear a sword for I am of a choleric nature," he would say with a grin.

He avoided social gatherings because, in his view, they tempted one to excess, idle talk, and detraction. Yet he would always welcome the poor at Morleys Hall, and at Christmas, Easter and Whitsun he would invite all comers to dinner, serving them himself and dining afterwards on whatever was left. Soup, boiled beef, goose and mince pies were regularly on the menu.

In showing this hospitality Ambrose was, of course, observing a Benedictine tradition. Whatever the difficulties, whatever the dangers, he was always a monk first and foremost. Nothing was allowed to interfere with his daily mental prayer and he would often say that he looked forward to this part of his day as worldly people looked forward to a feast.

When speaking to a woman he never looked at her directly, which some understandably found disconcerting. One lady asked him straight out why he was so chary of her sex since, after all, he had himself been born of a woman.

"For that very reason," replied Ambrose gravely, "that I was born of a woman."

Alcohol, also, he avoided almost completely—a more unusual thing in his day than in ours. He drank only beer which was scarcely fermented, and that very sparingly. "Wine and women make the wise apostatize," he would say.

On March 7, 1641, a government order warned all "Jesuits and seminary priests" to leave the country within one month, or suffer the penalty prescribed for traitors. A friend urged Ambrose, who was now seriously ill, at least to hide himself.

"Let them fear that have anything to lose that they are unwilling to part with," Ambrose responded.

A terrible shock had caused his stroke. Exactly what happened we will never know. According to his biographer he had learned that "some persons he loved as his own soul had resolved to do something very wicked which was likely to lead to the ruin of many souls."

His illness upset him deeply, for he feared that after his death there would be nobody to minister to his poor people. Needing the last sacraments, he could find no priest to administer them to him. Yet he carried on working and soon afterwards was arrested.

During the four months which he spent in Lancaster Castle awaiting trial a fellow Benedictine with influence at court asked him whether he would prefer to be sent into banishment or to be removed to London. Ambrose replied that he preferred neither and asked the monk not to trouble himself further about his welfare, since to die for the faith was to him more desirable than life.

The trial began on September 7, 1641. Ambrose at once admitted that he was a priest and that he had ministered in Lancashire for more than 20 years. Why, he was asked, had he not obeyed the government order and left the country? Ambrose pointed out that the order mentioned only Jesuits and seminary priests, and that he was neither. In any case, his illness had made such a journey impossible.

Mr. Justice Heath wanted to know what the prisoner thought of the laws under which priests were condemned to death. Ambrose replied bluntly that they were unjust and barbarous, and he pulled no punches in explaining why. And what, the judge persisted, of those who made and enforced those laws? Ambrose told him that he prayed that God would pardon them. He added a bold warning.

Ambrose: If, my Lord, in consequence of so unjust a law, you should condemn me to die, you would send me to heaven and yourself to hell.

Heath: Make what judgment you please of my salvation; for my part, though the law has brought you here as a criminal and a seducer of the people, I shall not pass so uncharitable a sentence on you.

Heath had orders from Parliament to see that any priest convicted at Lancaster paid the full penalty as "a terror to the Catholics who are numerous in that county." As we can see from his good-humored reply, Ambrose's courage and sincerity had impressed him favorably. Government orders notwithstanding, he would save his life if he could.

Telling Ambrose that his sickness excused him in

some measure, he offered to set him free if he promised to seduce the people no more. It would be easy to promise that, Ambrose replied, since he was no seducer but a reducer of the people to the ancient religion—and in that work he would continue until death.

Pilate-like, the astonished judge exclaimed, "You speak boldly to a man who is master of your life, and who can either acquit or condemn you as he shall judge proper."

In the world's eyes, replied Ambrose, Heath might indeed be an all-powerful judge. In spiritual matters, however, he himself, though a prisoner in the dock, was the real judge. And he warned Heath once more that by passing an unjust death sentence he would damn his own soul. At this point Heath's patience ran out.

"In that case," he retorted, "I shall have the advantage of you, since my sentence will be executed first."

Next day he ordered the jury to find Ambrose guilty and sentenced him to be hanged, drawn, and quartered. "Thanks be to God," replied Ambrose.

He prayed that God would pardon all who were responsible for his death, an act of charity, which won praise from the judge. He granted Ambrose's request for a private room in the castle where he might prepare himself for death.

Poor Sir Robert Heath! Like his predecessor Clench, who tried Margaret Clitherow, he strove hard with a prisoner who seemed determined to die. Who can help feeling a stab of pity for these decent but unheroic men, forced to administer laws which were not of their making and which they so obviously found distasteful!

Ambrose went to his death on September 10, 1641, carrying in his hands a little cross which he had fashioned for himself. After he had walked three times round the gallows, reciting the *Miserere,* he dealt brusquely with the Protestant ministers who were, inevitably, waiting to argue their case. Their challenge was, he told them, unseasonable and unfair. He had something else to do than listen to their fooleries.

When news of his death was sent to his brethren, the president general directed that, instead of the usual Requiem Masses, they should offer Masses of the Holy Trinity, sing the *Te Deum,* and perform other acts of thanksgiving.

14

The Merry Monk

Striding through the streets of St. Albans, Bartholomew Roe looked forward gleefully to an hour of honest fun. He liked arguing, and most of all he liked arguing with papists. A smart college man should soon have this one tied up in knots.

His opponent, indeed, was somewhat at a disadvantage, for he was presently a prisoner in the town jail. A humble mechanic by trade, he had broadcast his Catholic opinions too loudly and paid the inevitable penalty.

"The trouble with that fellow," said one disgruntled Protestant, "is that he knows more than is good for him. A few Scripture texts, a smattering of history picked up from some papist tract, and he thinks that he can outargue the Archbishop of Canterbury himself."

Bart Roe, on vacation from Cambridge, heard about the imprisoned papist when he came to St. Albans to visit his friends. There and then he made up his mind.

"I'll go over and see him," he said. "He won't outargue me."

His friends thought this a capital idea, not to say an amusing one. Bart Roe was one of the most brilliant young men on the Cambridge register. Poor Mr. David, muttering his popish prayers in his prison cell, would not last long against him.

The jail had once been the gatehouse of the ancient abbey, until Henry VIII had expelled the monks 70 years before. At least, thought Bart, his Catholic friend ought to feel at home here. Though it had been a prison for many years, the building still had a monkish feel.

The elderly turnkey led him down a damp corridor, unlocked a cell door, and pushed it open. Mr. David, a middle-aged man with gray hair and a kindly, humorous face, rose from a stool to greet him.

"I'm sorry to have to receive you here," he said with a smile. "When folk come to talk to me, I'm used to offering them some hospitality."

Bart liked the papist at once, and he could see that the feeling was returned. Here was no fanatic, just a decent, misguided man who had indeed read not wisely but too well. More than ever, Bart was glad that he had come. It was a shame that Mr. David should be locked up and he, Bart Roe, was going to obtain his release by showing him the error of his popish ways.

When Bart left the prison, many hours later, he knew for an absolute fact that Mr. David would be staying there for a long time to come. Not only had the Cambridge scholar failed to shake him; the poor mechanic had, with ruthless logic, bored such holes in his opponent's Protestant arguments that Bart, walking back slowly to his friend's house, now had grave doubts about the rightness of his own beliefs.

Transubstantiation, confession, the supremacy of the Pope—David had justified his belief in all of them, adroitly using reason, Scripture, and the Fathers of the

Church to prove his case. Several times Bart was driven into a corner as the gentle mechanic piled argument on argument, quotation on quotation. The whole experience had been shattering.

Back in Cambridge, among the books, Bart tried to find the answers to the doubts which the man had raised in his mind. The more he read, the more David seemed to be right.

Through Catholic friends he made contact with learned priests. Behind drawn curtains, by the light of guttering candles, their talks went on for hours into the night. Slowly, painfully, Bart faced the truth. The papists were right when they claimed that theirs was the one true Church.

News of Bartholomew Roe's conversion soon reached St. Albans, where the Protestant authorities were understandably furious. They had put David behind bars to stop him from talking popery, and he had inveigled this clever young man straight into the arms of Rome! The knave must be silenced, once and for all.

For a Catholic to convert a Protestant was a capital offence. David now found himself in the dock, facing the very real danger of the hangman's rope and the quartering block. Chief Justice Popham, that rabid Protestant, would gladly have sent him to the gallows, but the jury refused to convict. Could the mechanic be blamed if, in defending his religion, he had turned the tables on the scholar?

Having entered the Church, Bart quickly decided to become a priest and sailed for Douai. He arrived to find that he could not be admitted because the seminary was packed to the doors. After he had spent a few months in lodgings, however, a place was found for him and his studies began.

He had now begun to call himself Alban, in honor of

the town where he had been converted, and of the Roman soldier-saint who had been martyred there. Among his fellow students were at least two other men who would one day be canonized—Edmund Arrowsmith and Ambrose Barlow—and many more who were soon to give their lives for the faith.

Despite all this holiness and heroism, Douai seminary was not a serene place. There was much discontent among the students and quarrels with authority were frequent. (The English College in Rome had similar troubles). So turbulent was the atmosphere that Alban, like every other Douai student, was required to take an oath to do nothing deliberately to disturb the peace or discipline of the college.

He does not seem to have kept it very well. Indeed, it is quite clear that Alban Roe, forceful and outspoken, actually became a leader of the student unrest. On December 10, 1610, formal charges were laid against him:

"Having taken cousel and carefully examined the conduct of Mr. Bartholomew Roe, we the undersigned consider that the said Bartholomew is not at all fitted for the purpose of this college, on account of his contempt for the discipline and of his superiors and of his misleading certain youths living in the college, and also of the great danger of his still leading others astray. And therefore we adjudge that he must be dismissed from the college.

"For among other things the said Bartholomew Roe, when penance was given to certain students by their superior, publicly, and in the presence of many, blamed those who had performed the penance bestowed on them, saying, 'if it was my affair I should not have done the penance.' And another time he incited two youths not to submit to the punishment ordered by a superior, adding these and such-like expressions, 'Do you mean to submit to such an ignominious punishment?'

"He also untruly declared before the vice-president and the general prefect that it was not the president's intention that anyone should be punished for any reason by the loss of his portion of food, and also that it was not his intention that anyone should accuse another, or reveal another's offence, if he were asked by a superior if he knew of it.

"On another occasion, when a superior by the president's orders had removed from his bed place in the dormitory certain private cupboards, he answered him with contumacious words, saying, 'There is more trouble with a few fools than with all the wise; if you pull down, I will build up, if you destroy, I will rebuild.' "

The complaint, dated December 16, 1610, was signed by the vice-president and three of his professorial colleagues. In the New Year Alban got his marching orders.

He did not accept them quietly. On the following day he strode into the president's office with eight fellow students at his back, demanding that he be told why he was being dismissed. "When this uproar was quieted," says the official record, "the president refused to give his reasons."

That his superiors had cause to complain of Alban's behavior, we cannot doubt. Truculent and rebellious, he must have caused them many headaches and it seems reasonable that they should have sent him away until his attitude had changed.

The fault, however, was by no means all on Alban's side, nor was he the first student to be dismissed. Eight months earlier, for similar reasons, Thomas Maxfield had been sent back to England to mend his ways. Thomas, like Alban, eventually became a priest and suffered martyrdom with exceptional cheerfulness.

Alban left Douai amid further tumult from the

students, who protested that he had done no wrong and that even the college superiors, while they did not want him on the premises, had admitted that he was a fit candidate for ordination.

In fact, as a papal investigation found during the following year, Douai College was in a deplorable state. Incompetent management had brought morale to a very low ebb. Eventually the president, Dr. Worthington, was asked to resign. Under his successor, Dr. Kellison, matters slowly improved.

Almost certainly there was another unstated reason for the friction between Alban and his superiors— something more important than cupboards and penances. At Valladolid, as we have seen, the college authorities did not approve of their students becoming monks, and when the English Benedictines moved into Douai they met with even greater hostility. Until he was himself removed, Dr. Worthington did his best to drive them out of town.

The battle was at its hottest during Alban's time and although they never said so openly, it is a fair guess that Worthington and his colleagues feared that he was leading younger students towards the cloister. They may have been right, for no sooner had Alban left Douai than he entered the Order of St. Benedict.

The monastery, another English one, was founded at Dieulouard, in the diocese of Toul, by Father Augustine Bradshaw, whose friend Alban had become during his Douai days. The house was poor and strict, and it taught the young firebrand many lessons in humility and obedience without in any way damaging his bold spirit or the sense of humor which had made him so popular with his fellow students at the seminary.

Transferred to Paris, he was ordained in 1615 and sent to London, where he had much success in converting Protestants. Falling into the hands of the pursuivants, he was thrown into the New Prison in Maiden Lane. There he stayed for five years and suffered great hardships, until the Spanish ambassador, Count Gondomar, managed to get him released and banished.

He received the customary warning that he would die as a traitor if he dared to return, but that warning had not deterred others and it certainly did not deter Alban Roe. After a mere four months at Douai, he slipped back into England.

It was two years before he was captured once more. Alban Roe now found himself a prisoner in that very same jail at St. Albans where he had once gone to convert the mechanic David to Protestantism.

Whether he was working in Hertfordshire, or whether he was simply visiting, we do not know. We do know that here he suffered even more than during his earlier spell behind bars, for the prisoners were never allowed a fire and food had to be begged from passers-by. Alban, we are told, nearly perished from cold and hunger.

After two months in this sorry plight, friends had him transferred to London's Fleet prison. Here he was much better off. Indeed, he was scarcely a prisoner at all, for he was constantly allowed out and about on parole and so was able to carry on his ministry as before. This happy arrangement was, as we shall see, quite common during the reign of Charles I and his Catholic queen. St. John Southworth, whom we are to meet in the next chapter, also carried on a lively pastorate while officially a prisoner.

For 15 years Alban lived this strange life. Each evening he reported back to jail, where he constantly cheered up with his jokes the unlucky ones who really were prisoners. Good old Father Alban—always ready to enjoy a drink and a game of cards!

His convivial nature inevitably scandalized those for whom faith and fun were incompatible. In lugubrious Latin, a faceless secular priest complained formally about this monk who was so fond of wine bibbing and gambling. The complaint is suspect not least because in London, as abroad, the seculars frequently looked upon their Religious brethren with a jaundiced eye.

In 1640 the Long Parliament was summoned and the Puritan storm cloud gathered over the British Isles. Alban knew that civil war was coming and warned one of his brethren to prepare for it. Did he also realize that his own martyrdom was drawing near?

Before long he was transferred from the Fleet prison to Newgate and kept under close confinement—an ominous sign. On January 19, 1642, he was brought to the bar on charges of being a priest and of seducing Protestants from their religion.

Like Margaret Clitherow, Alban was unwilling that ignorant jurymen should have his death on their consciences. Like her, he at first refused to plead and was threatened with the *peine forte et dure,* the hideous crushing to death which she suffered.

Though Alban assured him that he was willing to suffer any pains for his Master's sake, the judge sent him back to jail for the night to think over the matter more carefully. Clench had given Margaret Clitherow a similar chance to change her mind.

Margaret had returned to the dock firm in her resolve. With Alban, it was different. Overnight he sought the opinion of priests—and presumably fellow prisoners—whom he considered more learned and more holy than himself. They advised him to plead not guilty and he took their advice.

Presumably Alban knew Margaret's story. Indeed, it

may well have been she who inspired his initial refusal. Their circumstances were not exactly similar, yet the moral problem appears fundamentally the same: should a martyr allow the innocent to be implicated in his, or her, death?

For whatever reasons, Margaret and Alban came to different conclusions and the Church has applauded both. Along with the 38 other martyrs featured in this book, the monk and the housewife were canonized together.

Of one thing we can be sure: Alban Roe was not afraid to die. Few martyrs, Thomas More not excepted, have faced the executioner so cheerfully.

A fallen Catholic, whom he had once helped, gave evidence against him. The sentence was inevitable. On his return to Newgate he preached a fervent sermon to the Catholics who had gathered there to get his blessing. He told them to welcome persecution as coming from the hand of God. Patience and resignation would win them greater glory. His one fear was that well-wishers would try to obtain his reprieve.

On the morning of his execution, January 21, he said Mass for a tiny congregation and gave them his last blessing.

"When you see our arms stretched out and nailed on the gates of the city," he told them, "think that we are giving you the same blessing that you now receive from us. And when you cast your eyes upon our heads, nailed up high on London Bridge, think that they are there to preach to you, and to proclaim that same holy faith for which we are about to die."

He spoke in plural because a companion was to travel with him to Tyburn. Father Thomas Reynolds, a secular priest, was over 80 years old. During half a century on the English mission he had weathered many a storm. Tried and condemned in 1628, he had

been reprieved at the queen's intercession and, like
Alban, allowed out of jail to carry on with his ministry.

Now, after 14 years, the sentence was to be carried
out. Poor Thomas was terrified and made no secret of
the fact.

It may seem strange that a man who had lived
dangerously for so long should quail at the last moment. At his age he could in any case hardly look
forward to many years of life. In fact, Thomas had
always been timid by nature—which makes his long
and perilous ministry all the more impressive.

God did not desert him now. He sent Alban Roe to
give him courage. As the moment to leave for Tyburn
drew near, he began to relax and even to smile at his
friend's jokes.

Alban came down to the hurdle with the air of a
conqueror, courteously saluted the sheriff and his
colleagues, and begged the crowd of weeping Catholics not to be distressed, for it was God's will that he
should leave them.

Lying down beside Thomas, who was already on the
hurdle, Alban took his hand and jokingly felt his pulse.

"Well, how do you find yourself now?" he asked
cheerily.

"In very good heart," the old man replied. "Blessed
be God for it, and I am glad to have for my comrade in
death a man of your undaunted courage."

They embraced one another, and the procession
started for Tyburn.

An eyewitness on the route wrote afterwards:

> It is almost incredible how Protestants and Catho-
> lics made towards these blessed martyrs, as they were
> drawn through the streets on the hurdle. Some were
> kissing their hands and some their garments, others
> craving their blessings publicly, others saying, 'Cour-
> age, valiant soldiers of Christ.' And the martyrs on the

other side bade them joyfully farewell, saying they more esteemed it to be drawn up Holborn on a sledge for this cause than if they were riding in the best coach the king had, and that they were going to a marriage feast."

In the crowd Alban spotted the manservant of one of his friends.

"Remember me to your master," he called, "and tell him that you met me riding in a cart without wheels, and that I am going to a place where, as I hope, I shall pray for him."

Despite their good spirits, it was not a comfortable journey. The route that day was covered with mud and puddles and their clothes and faces were much splashed with dirt.

During a halt Catholics stepped forward to beg some souvenir from Alban. He gave them his handkerchief and everything else that he had in his pockets.

"Come, whip up now!" he shouted to the carter gaily when he had nothing left.

Amazed at his kindness and good humor, Protestants began to murmur that perhaps his religion was the true one after all. Others said boldly that they would become Catholics no matter what the consequences might be.

Continually on this last journey Alban thought of others. When a poor workingman stepped forward to bid him farewell, Alban could see that he was distressed.

"Friend, don't be dismayed to see me here," he told him gently, "but know that I am on my way to a great feast."

At last they arrived at Tyburn and were unbound from the hurdle. Three felons were to die with them; one of these Alban had reconciled to the Church while they were in prison. After he had comforted and absolved the man, the two martyrs made their last confessions to each other, embraced and exchanged congratulations. Then they kissed the ropes hanging from the gallows and put them on as though they were stoles.

Thomas spoke from the cart for a good half hour, praying for a good end to the dispute between king and Parliament, and that their innocent blood should not lie heavy upon England. Courteous to the last, he turned to the official in charge of the execution.

"God bless you, Mr. Sheriff," he concluded, "and reward you for your goodness towards me, and for your patience in bearing with my tediousness, and grant you his grace to make you a glorious saint in heaven."

Baring his head, the sheriff answered in a low voice, "And I commend myself to you."

Thomas, who had been so afraid, reduced the sheriff to tears with his courage. A veteran of many executions, he told colleagues that never had he known a man meet death in such a fashion. As for the crowd, they were as silent as though in church.

Then it was Alban's turn, and immediately the atmosphere changed. Stepping forward, he looked around him with a smile.

"Well, here's a jolly company!" he exclaimed.

He did not speak for long, explaining that Thomas had uttered most of his thoughts for him. He offered his death for his sins and forgave his persecutors. Then he, too, turned to the sheriff.

"Pray, sir," he said, "if I conform to your religion and go to church, will you secure my life?"

"That I will!" replied the sheriff with feeling, "upon my word, my life for yours if you will do but that!"

"See then," said Alban to the crowd, "what the crime is for which I am to die, and whether my religion be not my only treason."

The Protestant minister, whose usual task was to badger the condemned man with argument, played no such role at this execution. Alban could see that, like everyone else, the man was much moved.

"I will remember you," Alban told him.

"I pray you will," replied the minister.

When someone offered him a handkerchief for his face, Alban declined politely. The cause for which he was to die was, he said, so good and glorious that he did not fear to look death in the face, nor to be seen by the crowd.

After they had prayed for a while, Alban rose up and spotted one of the turnkeys who had known him in the Fleet prison.

"My friend, I find thou art a prophet," he called, eyes twinkling. "Thou hast told me often that I should be hanged, and truly my unworthiness was such I could not believe it, but I see that thou art a prophet."

To the hangman he gave money for a drink, bidding him serve God and not get drunk. As the man bound them, Alban urged him gaily, "Let all be secure and do thy duty neatly; I have been a neat man all my life!"

They were allowed to hang until they were dead, Alban being seen to spread his hands apart and put them together as though praying. Then came the butchery and with it the scramble for relics—some of them preserved to this day.

15

When the Plague Raged

Dipping his thumb into the holy oil, Henry Morse turned to the young woman who lay, covered with sacking, on a filthy straw mattress in the tiny tenement room.

"Through this holy anointing and his most tender mercy may the Lord forgive you whatever sins you have committed. . . ."

Carefully, Henry anointed eyelids ravaged by the plague. Always, at this moment, Henry had to steel himself. He must not flinch or grimace, must not let Jane see, even by a flicker, how much it revolted him to touch those ugly, suppurating carbuncles which covered her head and face. Only a few days ago she had been the lively, attractive mother of two tiny children. Her husband, a hard working stonemason, was kind to her and brought home his wages each week instead of spending them in the alehouse. Now he and the children were dead, and before morning Jane's plague-ridden body would follow theirs into the common pit.

Ears, nostrils, mouth, hands, feet—the disease had touched them all. Indeed, it had spared no part of her. Yet Henry anointed the girl as gently and reverently as he would the queen herself, murmuring each blessing in a clear, calm voice.

As the girl looked up at him with trusting eyes, Henry thought with shame of the days when he had first come into these fetid slums to care for the plague victims. Sensitive and fastidious by nature, he had so feared to touch those horrible sores that he had often fled from the premises as soon as he had heard the patient's confession and given him Holy Communion, leaving him to die unanointed.

His colleague, Father John Southworth, had denounced his cowardice to his superiors with Lancashire bluntness. Henry, ashamed, had omitted the anointing no more.

From the fireplace a cloud of black smoke billowed into the room, and with it an acrid stench which made Henry catch his breath. Jane's elderly mother-in-law, poking and muttering, had thrown an old boot which had belonged to her son on to the pile of blazing logs.

"'Twill help kill the pestilence," she murmered. Fighting down his nausea, Henry smiled and nodded. He knew that the old woman, confused and senile, had not yet fully comprehended the deaths of her son and grandchildren, and did not realize that Jane, too, was about to die.

The heat in the room was almost unbearable, for although the night outside was stifling, the doors and windows were firmly shut. Rich people burned tar and niter to disinfect the air, believing that the disease travelled through it. The poor, unable to afford such luxury, used scraps of horn and leather instead. The old woman poked the boot once more, grunting with satisfaction as a fresh smoke cloud billowed forth.

With a few parting words of encouragement and hope, Henry picked up his white wand and his hat, and stepped out into the garbage-strewn street. The wand, like the plague badge on his coat, warned his healthy fellow citizens that he was in constant contact with the disease. Most heeded the warning and gave him a wide berth.

Ahead of him a death cart rumbled through the dusk. As Henry breathed in the night air the cart stopped and its two attendants, weirdly masked against the pestilence, hurried into a tenement whose door had been hurriedly flung open. Within a few seconds they were out in the street again, carrying between them the naked body of a boy no more than 12 years old. Without ceremony they flung it into the cart, and the lumbering horse moved on. Within an hour, Henry told himself, the cart would be full.

The plague which raged through 1636 was not the first which London had seen, nor would it be the last. In an alleyway off Fleet Street a three-year-old boy named Samuel Pepys, son of a poor tailor, now gazed with a child's bewildered eyes on sights which he was to describe vividly and for all time when he saw them again 30 years later.

During Queen Elizabeth's reign, and for many years afterwards, London plague victims received the sacraments from any priest who might be available. As the epidemics grew in number and intensity, it became clear that if all priests were exposed to the risk of infection, there might soon be none left to minister to anyone.

If was therefore agreed that two priests, one Jesuit and one secular, should be appointed chaplains to the plague-stricken. The Jesuits chose Henry Morse, the seculars John Southworth. Both were to die, not of the plague, but as martyrs at Tyburn.

Like his Jesuit namesake Henry Walpole, young Henry Morse began his career as a law student at London's Inns of Court. Raised in Suffolk as a Protestant, he soon found that the claims of the Catholic Church were pushing statutes and cases out of his head. Convinced that those claims were valid, he took ship for Douai, was received into the Church and returned to England, to be promptly jailed. Before long, however, he was released and banished. Back at Douai, he entered the seminary, transferring later to Rome.

Ordained a secular priest, he reentered England via Newcastle and for two years worked among the dockers and miners of Northumberland and Durham. In 1626 he was again arrested, and spent the next three years in that same York Castle where Henry Walpole had been held.

During her time there Margaret Clitherow had felt herself to be part of a religious community, so devout was the shared life of the Catholic prisoners. In York Castle Henry Morse actually became a Religious, performing his novitiate in the Society of Jesus under a fellow prisoner who was a Jesuit priest.

Freed and banished once more, he worked in the Low Countries as a chaplain to English soldiers fighting for the king of Spain. For a time he also served in Jesuit houses at Watten and Liege.

During this period he had his first serious illness, a fever from which he recovered. Though never strong afterwards, he returned to England—to London and the plague.

Henry's "parish" was a network of slums around Westminster Abbey and St. Martin-in-the-Fields, in the area where Trafalgar Square and Nelson's column now stand. Here he looked after 400 families, Catholic and Protestant alike, distributing food and medicines along with spiritual care.

This terrible disease, carried from the East by fleas on the backs of ship-borne rats, brought a host of added sufferings in its wake. Once it had broken out Londoners became prisoners within their own city, and the sick became prisoners within their own homes. Anyone with the dreaded swellings upon him was hanged as a felon if he tried to flee. Other would-be fugitives were whipped.

When the family breadwinner was stricken, extreme poverty swiftly followed. On October 6, 1636, Henry and John made a public appeal which showed how desperate was the need:

"There are some persons in the number of those afflicted who, notwithstanding they were well born and bred, have been constrained through extremity of want to sell or pawn all they had, remain shut up within the bare walls of a poor chamber, having not wherewithal to allay the pangs of hunger, nor scarcely cover nakedness. There are others who, for the space of three days together, have not gotten a morsel of bread to put into their mouths. We have just cause to fear that some do perish for want of food; others for want of tendance; others for want of ordinary helps and remedies. . . ."

The plight of Catholic victims was particularly grave, since their religion barred them from receiving the relief handed out by Anglican parish officials. Their names did not appear on the register, so officially they did not exist. Urging more fortunate Catholics to be generous, the two priests quote some outstanding Protestant benefactions. Members of the one true Church should not, they suggest, be outdone in charity by heretical neighbors.

During much of Charles I's reign the laws against

priests were not rigidly enforced and the two went about their heroic work with little or no harassment. If, however, some bigoted or money-grubbing informer chose to denounce a particular priest, authority was forced to act.

In the first days of 1638 Henry was confronted in the street by a professional priest catcher named John Cook, who threatened to turn him in unless he paid a ransom of five pounds. Henry realized at once that the five pounds would be a mere starter; when it was spent, Cook would be back for more.

However, he took the rogue with him to the house of a Catholic cutler named William Hodson, whom Henry knew he could rely on for help. Promising to take Cook to the local tavern, where payment would be made over a drink, William went upstairs on the pretext of borrowing the cash from two friends.

When they learned what was afoot, the friends drew their swords and made for the door, determined to skewer the blackmailer where he stood. It was with difficulty that Henry restrained them.

The plague had now died down and the need of his poor people was no longer so great. Realizing that he could not hope to raise enough money to buy safety for himself, Henry surrendered to the authorities.

His heroism had brought a rich harvest of converts among the Protestants whom he tended. Naturally this rankled. At his trial Henry was accused of having "seduced" no fewer than 560 souls to the Roman religion. The figure may not have been far wrong.

Though found guilty of being a priest, he was not sentenced to death. Queen Henrietta, a Frenchwoman and a devout Catholic, persuaded her husband to release him on bail of 10,000 florins. For the next three years Henry worked quietly among the Catholics of Devon and Cornwall.

The edict of March, 1641, which banished all priests on pain of death, presented him with an agonizing decision. He did not want to leave England, yet if he stayed, his sureties might be made to forfeit their bail. After much prayer, he sailed once more for the Low Countries and another stint as an army chaplain.

Though here, too, he was a success and made many converts, Henry was soon begging his superior to send him back to England. In 1643 they gave in. Overjoyed, Henry went from room to room in the Jesuit house at Ghent, telling his colleagues that he was going home to die for the faith.

He was appointed this time to work among the Catholics of Cumberland, in the northwest corner of the country. Though England was now a dangerous place indeed for a Catholic priest, he dodged the Puritans successfully for 18 months. Then, riding late one night to answer a sick call, he walked into a troop of Parliamentarian soldiers.

They were actually looking for someone else, but they suspected at once that Henry was a priest. Placing him under arrest, they set out for the jail at Durham.

During the long journey through the war ravaged countryside, the troops lodged their prisoner overnight at the house of a local constable. Here, to Henry's surprise, the lady of the house treated him as though he were an honored guest rather than a suspected traitor. Her manner was courteous, even deferential, contrasting strangely with the gruffness of her husband and the Roundhead soldiers.

With her husband absent, she began to despatch the servants one by one on various errands, until at last she faced Henry alone.

"Are you a priest?" she asked softly.

Henry, returning her gaze, did not reply. He had

guessed that she was almost certainly a Catholic—but could he be sure? Was this a trap, sprung by his captors to trick him into admitting his priesthood?

Something in the woman's eyes gave him confidence.

"I am a priest," he replied.

His hostess smiled.

"I knew it, from the moment I saw you," she told him.

The escape plan was ready. While the servants were away, she would smuggle him out of the house and take him by little-used paths to a meeting place where Catholic friends, already alerted, would be waiting to hide him.

Filled with wonder and gratitude, Henry was nevertheless troubled.

"Surely, by helping me to escape, you will bring suffering upon yourself," he objected.

"Whether I will suffer is not certain," she replied. "What is certain is that I would rather lose everything—home, family, life itself—rather than hand over an innocent man, and a priest at that, to his enemies."

So Henry and his brave rescuer stole out into the night, bidding each other farewell at the crossroads where shadowy figures waited in the trees.

For the next six weeks Henry lay low, while the fury of England's civil war raged around his hiding place. The Roundheads were laying siege to Newcastle, the port on which London relied for its coal supplies. In the end the king's forces surrendered and Cromwell was a step nearer to victory.

He dared not remain too long in one place, Henry knew that. Apart from the danger to himself, he was putting too great a strain on the folk who were hiding him. The time had come to move on.

His guide, a local man, knew the moorland well and had led others across it by night as he now led Henry.

"Not far to go now," he murmured, as they came to a winding road over the fells.

"How far?" asked Henry.

"A mile, no more."

In silence they struck out along the rough highway. Tired and cold, Henry would be glad to reach his destination. Suddenly the guide stopped and put a hand to his head. A bewildered look passed over his face.

"What is it?" asked Henry.

"I . . . I can't remember the way."

He blurted out the words as though he could not himself believe what he was saying.

"But I thought. . . "

"I know how to get there—I must know!" the guide exclaimed desperately. "But I can't remember. It's as though I have lost my memory."

Below them, in a tiny hollow, a light gleamed.

"Perhaps the house is yonder," Henry suggested.

"If not, there'll be somebody there who can put us on the right road," said the guide.

Henry could see that his friend was worried. His strange lapse of memory had unnerved him, and they both knew that to knock at the cottage was to arouse suspicion. In these troubled times nobody ventured out at night without serious cause.

Their footsteps, crunching on the path, brought the cottager to the door. He was a Puritan—the harsh set of the mouth and the dark clothes told them at once. A middle-aged man with grizzled hair, he awaited them, motionless and impassive. Behind him in the doorway stood his two sons, burly, hard-eyed young fellows, one fingering a blunderbuss.

"We are lost, friend," began the guide nervously, "and we hoped you might be able to set us on our way."

"Set you on your way," replied the cottager. "Aye, I'll do that all right."

Henry tried to stand back in the shadow, but the man's gaze bored into his face and the Puritan mouth curled in something like a sneer.

"Aren't you," he said slowly, "the man who lately escaped from the soldiers while they were carrying you to Durham?"

So it was over. It was no use to bluff. The man recognized him, had seen him before; where, Henry could not tell. Perhaps he had watched from those hard Puritan eyes, satisfaction on his face, as Henry was marched through the nearby village to the constable's house.

"Well?"

As the Puritan took a pace forward, the blunderbuss was slowly levelled at Henry's chest.

He could not hope to flee into the darkness; he would be shot before he had gone a yard. In any case, he now realized, he did not want to escape. He had come to England to die for his faith, and clearly it was God's will that die he should. This was the meaning of the guide's loss of memory, the reason why their footsteps had led to the house of the enemy.

Henry stepped forward and faced all three. To their astonishment, he was smiling.

"Yes," he answered, "I am that man."

They took him back to London on a coal ship, where the black dust covered him and the sailors swore and struck at him. Then a storm blew up, so fierce that it silenced their curses and reduced them to white-faced terror. Tossed and buffetted, they watched helpless as a sister ship sailing close to them sank beneath the giant waves. Of all those on board, only Henry was not afraid.

When his brother, an eminent lawyer and a Protestant, heard that he was captured once more and a prisoner in Newgate, he used every ounce of his skill and influence in an effort to save Henry's life. It was all in vain. Henry had been convicted once already of being a priest. Now, without further trial, he was sentenced to die.

On the morning of his execution, February 1,1645, he rose early and celebrated a votive Mass of the Holy Trinity. At nine o'clock the sheriff came to the prison and courteously handed him down to the sledge, on which grass had been spread to make his journey more comfortable. His services during the plague had not been entirely forgotten.

On the way to Tyburn the French ambassador, riding in his coach, stepped down to beg his blessing and his prayers for the kingdom of France. Then, complete with coach and retinue, he accompanied Henry to the gallows, giving his journey the air of a triumphal procession.

The usual large crowd awaited him, many of them Catholics with rosaries to bless and coins for him to bite on as souvenirs. He addressed them briefly and modestly, offering his death as an atonement for the sins of the nation.

As the cart was driven away, an urchin jumped forward and swung on his legs. Soldiers and officials cuffed the lad away—but not too quickly.

The fate of Henry Morse did not, of course, deter John Southworth from his own ministry among the London poor. We first met John briefly in the previous chapter, giving absolution to Edmund Arrowsmith as he left Lancaster Castle for his execution.

The Southworths were yet another of those brave recusant families with which Lancashire was studded. Like the Arrowsmiths and the Barlows, they had already suffered much when John was born in 1592. Their home, Samlesbury Hall, may be seen today, standing by the roadside a few miles from Blackburn.

The countryside around is still green and rural, looking much as it must have done when, at the age of 21, John bade it farewell and set out for Douai. Ordained five years later, he tried his vocation as a Benedictine but found that he was not called to be a monk. By the end of the year 1619 he was working in London as a secular priest.

Five years after that he returned to Douai, then spent a brief period in Brussels as confessor to Benedictine nuns. Why he left England at this time we do not know. Information about John's missionary career is sparse. Possibly London had become too hot for him, for when he did slip back into the country he kept clear of the capital and headed home to Lancashire.

In 1627 he was arrested and charged with being a priest on English soil. Sentenced to death, he was reprieved but not released. It was at this time that he bade his poignant farewell to Edmund Arrowsmith.

After three years John was transferred from Lancaster to the Clink prison in London. There, at Queen Henrietta's intercession, he was released to the custody of the French ambassador along with 15 other priests, all of them being ordered to leave the country forthwith.

It is unlikely that John obeyed the order, for two years later he was back in prison. It was not a rigorous confinement. The Puritan writer Prynne complained bitterly that "he had full liberty to walk abroad at his pleasure as most priests had during their imprisonment." John was, in fact, technically a prisoner during the period when he and Henry Morse were working so devotedly for the plague victims.

Like his Jesuit colleague, John enjoyed great success as a convert maker. An outraged Anglican cleric, Robert White, petitioned to have the crafty papist put back behind bars. White was stationed at St. Margaret's, a church which nestles in the shadow of Westminster Abbey and is today known for its society weddings. His address to the authorities, written in 1640, fairly splutters with indignation:

> "This man, under pretense of distributing alms . . . doth take occasion to go into the houses of one William Baldwin and William Stiles in the Kemp Yard in Westminster, and there finding Baldwin near the point of death, did set upon him by all means to make him change his religion; whereunto by his subtle persuasions, Baldwin easily consented and received the sacrament from him, according to the Church of Rome, and so died a Romish Catholic. And Southwell (*sic*), to color and hide these wicked practices, doth feed the watchman and other poor people thereabouts, etc. And thus, under a pretense of relieving the bodies of poor people, he poisons their souls."

Since some of the alms which John distributed came from the queen herself, White did not have much chance of stopping his ministry. For a brief time he was put back in his cell, but Her Majesty soon had him out again.

Of John's life during the next 14 years we know nothing. Presumably he continued to work quietly in London and may well have been in the crowd which, on a January day in 1649, saw Charles I die by the headsman's axe in Whitehall.

One night in 1654, a posse of soldiers under a Colonel Windlesham burst into John's room as he lay asleep and placed him under arrest. A pursuivant named Jefferies, probably out to make money, had laid information against him.

Like Margaret Clitherow and Ambrose Barlow, John was given every opportunity to save his life; like them, he refused to do so. Under interrogation he had at once admitted being a priest. His judges would not have this admission read into the record. For hours they did their utmost to persuade him to plead not guilty. If he would do so, urged the judge, his life would be safe. There was no other evidence which proved his priesthood.

John, who was now 72 years old, steadfastly turned aside all their well-meant arguments. To deny that he was a priest would, he said, be to deny his religion, and that he would never do.

Realizing that they could not deter him, they were compelled to let the law take its course. When the time came to pass sentence the recorder of London, Serjeant Steel, was so overcome by tears that it was some time before he could get the words out.

June 28, 1654, was a day of storm and rain, yet thousands of people, with many coaches and horses, gathered to witness the execution of John Southworth. The Catholic ambassadors had pleaded with Cromwell for his life, but the protector refused mercy to the man who had toiled so long and so bravely among the London poor. John was dragged to Tyburn to die with five coiners.

Wearing his cassock and biretta, he was helped into the cart and began, in a firm voice, his farewell speech to the crowd:

"Good people, I was born in Lancashire. This is the third time I have been apprehended, and now being to die, I would gladly witness and profess openly my faith, for which I suffer. And though my time be short, yet what I shall be deficient in words I hope I shall supply with my blood, which I will most willingly spend to the last drop for my faith. Neither my intent in coming into England, nor practice in England, was to act anything against the secular government. Hither I was sent by my lawful superiors to teach Christ's faith, not to meddle with any temporal affairs. Christ sent his apostles; his apostles their successors; and their successors me."

Blunt to the last, John reminds his audience that Cromwell and his men marched to war with liberty of conscience as their battle cry. Yet now that they are in power, they see no wrong in persecuting Catholics and executing a priest, simply for using that selfsame liberty:

"My faith is my crime, the performance of my duty the occasion of my condemnation. I confess I am a great sinner; against God I have offended but am innocent of any sin against man; I mean the Commonwealth and present government. How justly then I die, let them look to who have condemned me. It is sufficient for me that it is God's will: I plead not for myself (I came here to suffer), but for you poor Catholics whom I leave behind me.

"Heretofore liberty of conscience was pretended as a cause of war; and it was held a reasonable proposition that all the natives should enjoy it, who should be found to behave themselves as obedient and true subjects. This being so, why should their conscientious acting and governing themselves, according to the faith received from their ancestors, involve them more than all the rest in an universal guilt?

"It has pleased God to take the sword out of the king's hand and put it in the protector's. Let him remember that he is to administer justice indifferently and without exception of persons. For there is no exception of persons with God, whom we ought to resemble."

When all was over the Spanish ambassador bought the hacked-up body from the hangman for 40 shillings, had the quarters stitched together by a surgeon, and then had them embalmed. The body was presented to John's old college at Douai, where it was laid near the altar.

In 1793, at the outbreak of the French Revolution, students hastily buried the body as the revolutionary troops arrived to seize the college. Its resting place was forgotten.

In 1927 the old college building was demolished to make way for a new road to the present railway station. A workman, digging out the foundations, suddenly came upon a coffin.

The local antiquarian society sent news of the discovery to England. The body was x-rayed and found to have been quartered. The head was in a good state of preservation, the lips slightly parted as in a peaceful smile.

On April 30, 1930, the body of John Southworth was carried into Westminster Cathedral, escorted by hundreds of priests, heads of Religious Orders, and all the Bishops of England and Wales. And there it lies today, covered in silver and dressed in the red vestments of martyrdom, on the site of those very streets through which he used to hurry to the aid of the dying.

16
The Big Lie

In the fall of the year 1678, a shiver of terror ran through Protestant England. The papists, so far tolerantly treated during Charles II's reign, had hatched a vast conspiracy to kill the king and put his brother, the Catholic duke of York, on the throne.

There were, it appeared, three alternative schemes afoot. Sir George Wakeman, the queen's physician, was to poison the merry monarch for a consideration of 15,000 pounds. If Sir George failed in his mission, four Irish ruffians would be hired to stab Charles at Windsor. And if that, too, proved unworkable, two Jesuits named Grove and Pickering were to shoot him with a bullet fashioned from silver in deference to his royal status.

Titus Oates, to whom the nation was indebted for uncovering the dreadful plot, was a squat bull of a man whose head appeared to grow out of his shoulders. Son of an Anabaptist preacher, he was expelled successively from school and from two Cambridge colleges, where, according to a contemporary, "he was a great dunce, ran into debt and, being sent away for want of money, never took a degree."

Despite this unpromising start, Oates was ordained as an Anglican cleric but quickly found himself in jail for his first essay in perjury—scandalous and unfounded charges against a schoolmaster whose place he coveted. Before he could be tried, he escaped and sought refuge as chaplain to a man-of-war in Tangier.

Dismissed from this post, he managed to secure a place as chaplain to the Protestants in the household of the Catholic duke of Norfolk. In this atmosphere he conceived the idea which was to make him a national hero and the judicial murderer of at least 35 innocent people.

The man who inspired him was Israel Tonge, a fanatical anti-Jesuit, with whom he made friends at this time. Without Tonge behind him, it is doubtful whether Oates would ever have been able to carry the plan through. At Tonge's suggestion he became a Catholic and went to Valladolid, ostensibly to study for the priesthood but in fact to spy there. His low moral character got him expelled within five months, so he moved on to France and the seminary of St. Omer, which also saw him off in short order.

Back in London he started to hang about such Catholic haunts as the Pheasant, in Holborn. In this way he was able to pick up sufficiently detailed gossip to lend the color of truth to his lies later on.

On September 28, 1678, he made a sworn statement before a magistrate, Sir Edmund Berry Godfrey. When the king had been assassinated, he alleged, his councillors were also to be killed and a French army would invade Ireland. There would then be a general massacre of Protestants. To make all this possible, vast sums had been provided by Jesuits and Benedictines on the Continent.

Final details of the plot had been arranged, according to Oates, at a secret meeting of Jesuits held on April 24 that year in the White Horse Tavern in Fleet Street. The Jesuits did indeed meet in the tavern on this date, but only for their triennial congregation.

Having spun his wild tale, Oates had an enormous stroke of luck. Sir Edmund, the magistrate who had taken his statement, was found dead in a ditch, face down and transfixed by his own sword, in circumstances never explained. It was at once assumed, without a single shred of evidence, that Catholics had murdered him.

The flames of hysteria were fanned with gusto by the earl of Shaftesbury, who was anxious to exclude James as heir apparent. When Oates appeared before the Privy Council he found everyone eager to believe him but the king himself. Charles, a weak ruler but no fool, cross-examined him carefully and detected a number of misstatements and inconsistencies in his story. He openly called Oates a lying scoundrel, but it made no difference. England was now firmly in the grip of anti-Catholic fever, and the terror was on.

Hailed as the savior of the nation, Oates was granted a pension by Parliament and provided with a permanent bodyguard. A duke was appointed to superintend his safety and other court officials to see to his household needs.

Flanked by his guards, a squad of pursuivants at his back, he strutted about London in bishop's robes, striking fear into all hearts. "Whoever he pointed at was taken up and committed," wrote a contemporary, "and people got out of his way as from a blast."

One of his earliest victims, a Benedictine lay brother named Thomas Pickering, was known to the king personally. Presumably he was the "Jesuit" named by Oates in his original statement. When he was brought before the Council, Charles asked him bluntly:

"Is it you, Pickering, who wish to shoot me with a pistol?"

"No, sire," replied Thomas, "I have never fired a pistol in my life."

"I thought so," the king replied.

The queen, who was also present, treated the charge scathingly. Gazing at the gentle monk, she declared, "I should have more fear to be alone in my chamber with a mouse."

During his long exile on the Continent, Charles II had received much kindness from the English Benedictines. Yet two months later, along with two priests, Blessed Thomas Pickering was hanged.

The national panic, spreading to every quarter of the realm, provided a marvellous opportunity both for fanatics and for those with private grudges to settle. Father John Plessington had quietly exercised his ministry for many years, first at Holywell, in North Wales, and then at Puddington, in Cheshire, where he lived with the Massey family.

We know little about him save that his family came from the same part of Lancashire as John Southworth and gave its name to a village which still exists. Born near Garstang, some little distance away, John received his early education from the Jesuits in his home county, studied for the priesthood at Valladolid, and was ordained in 1662.

Of John, Bishop Challoner writes, "His zeal in his function, joined to a certain candor and agreeableness in conversation, as it made him esteemed and loved by the good, so it raised him enemies among those who were not good." In other words, like Ambrose Barlow and John Southworth he combined great holiness with a blunt Lancashire tongue, and it made him enemies.

The three witnesses who appeared against him—

Margaret Platt, George Massey and Robert Wood— were all renegade Catholics. The trial took place at Chester and it was in that picturesque little city, still surrounded by its Roman wall, that John Plessington was dragged out to die.

He is chiefly remembered for the simple farewell address which he gave to the crowd on that far-off July day in 1679:

> "Dear countrymen, I am here to be executed, neither for theft, murder, nor anything against the law of God, nor any fact or doctrine inconsistent with monarchy or civil government. . . . Nothing was laid to my charge but priesthood."

If to be a Catholic priest is to be a traitor, he asks, what must become of the Anglican clergy? Did not the first Protestant bishops receive their ordination from those of the Church of Rome?

> "That the Pope hath power to depose or give license to murder princes, is no part of our belief. And I protest in the sight of God and the court of heaven, that I am innocent of the plot so much discoursed of, and abhor such bloody and damnable designs."

Yet he is neither afraid nor bitter, but glad to die for his faith and in atonement for his sins:

> "I have deserved a worse death, for though I have been a faithful and true subject to my king, I have been a grievous sinner against God. Thieves and robbers that rob on highways would have served God in a greater perfection than I have done, had they received so many favors and graces from Him as I have. . . .
>
> "Bear witness, good hearers, that I profess that I undoubtedly and firmly believe all the articles of the Roman Catholic faith, and for the truth of any of them, by the assistance of God, I am willing to die; and I had rather die than doubt any point of faith taught by our Holy Mother, the Roman Catholic Church."

Before he died, John Plessington made it clear while forgiving those who had sworn away his life, that some at least of the evidence was false. Of these witnesses one was crushed to death by an accident not long afterwards, another died in a hog sty, and the third "lingered away in anguish and misery."

Philip Evans was playing tennis when a grave-faced jailer brought him the news. Against all expectations, the court's sentence had been confirmed. Philip and John Lloyd, the priest condemned with him, were to die next day.

So broad was Philip's smile that the jailer wondered whether he had understood. Gently he suggested that the young Jesuit return to his cell.

"What haste is there?" demanded Philip cheerfully. "Let me play out my game first!"

With that, he turned and served another ball.

So sure were the authorities at Cardiff Castle that Philip and John would be reprieved, they regularly allowed them out of their cells and even out of the castle limits, during their 11-week wait for the royal decision. There had, after all, been the utmost difficulty in getting witnesses to testify against them. Several men had been flogged for refusing to admit that they had seen them officiating as priests—one so severely that he died.

In the end a poor old woman and her daughter had been suborned to give the necessary testimony, together with a dwarf by the name of Mayne Trott. Mr. Justice Logher was not impressed with their performance.

"If you believe what the women have said," he told the jury laconically, "it is your duty to pronounce a verdict of guilty."

A juryman, Richard Bassett by name, snapped his fingers.

"You can leave that to us. By God, we shall find them guilty!" he retorted. And so they did.

Born in Monmouthshire in 1645, Philip Evans went to school at St. Omer, joined the Society of Jesus and was ordained at Liege, Belgium, when he was 30. He possessed, according to his provincial, "a wonderful frankness of disposition, and a pleasant unclouded countenance, with a brow always free from furrows."

Sent back immediately to work in South Wales, he refused the urgent pleading of friends who wanted him to fly from the Titus Oates terror. Nothing would make him give up his flock, or the post which his superiors had assigned to him. Meanwhile, a fanatical Abergavenny magistrate named John Arnold was hunting high and low for Philip, and offering 200 pounds reward for his capture.

Caught and thrown into the castle of Cardiff, he was kept for three weeks in solitary confinement in an underground dungeon. Then John Lloyd, a secular priest, came to join him.

Philip must have been overjoyed, for here was a man very like himself, though, we shall see, John was the less extrovert of the two. Nevertheless, his innocence and humility made him popular with everyone who knew him. Born in Brecknockshire, he had studied in Ghent and Valladolid, where he was ordained in 1653.

Philip and John were, as we have seen, tried together. When they were sentenced Philip bowed to judge and jury, thanking them all and naming particularly the blackguard Bassett. On the night before the execution, after finishing his game, he played on his harp and spoke joyfully with the large number of people who came to say good-bye.

To fasten Philip in irons now was a particularly stupid act of cruelty, for he had resolutely turned his back on every opportunity to run away. In the morning it took the smith an hour to remove the shackles and in doing so he caused Philip considerable pain. Yet still he did not complain. He simply encouraged the man to do his work and not to fear hurting him.

The condemned priests were taken to Gallows Field in a cart on July 22, 1679. When they arrived, Philip told the crowd, "Sure this is the best pulpit a man can have to preach in, therefore I cannot forbear to tell you again that I die for God and religion's sake, and I think myself so happy that if I had never so many lives, I would willingly give them all for so good a cause."

Though still a young man, he told them, he would really live only a little time even if he were spared. He was, therefore, happy to purchase with a short pain an everlasting life.

He forgave all who had played any part in his death and thanked those who had been kind to him. Then he turned to the friend beside him. "Adieu, Mr. Lloyd," he said, "though for a little time, for we shall shortly meet again."

John addressed the crowd only briefly because, as he pointed out, Philip had already spoken for both of them. "Besides," he added, "I never was a good speaker in my life."

Like Philip he forgave his enemies, thanked those who had been kind, and died uttering a simple prayer.

For John Wall, with 22 years on the English mission behind him, the Titus Oates terror was simply a return to the kind of persecution which he had known long before. Once, at King's Norton, near Birmingham, he had had an extremely narrow escape from capture. The man who helped him to escape was a Protestant named Thomas Milward, who hid the Franciscan in his house while the pursuivants went off in the wrong direction.

"If it please God that I have to die for the faith," John promised him afterwards, "I will offer my life's blood for your soul."

Yet another son of Catholic Lancashire, John Wall was born near Preston in 1620. Trained for the priesthood in Douai and Rome, he was ordained at 25 and joined the Franciscans six years later, taking the name Father Joachim of St. Anne. So impressed were his superiors by the young priest's ability and zeal that within a year he had been appointed vicar of the Douai community and novice master as well.

In 1656, during Cromwell's reign, he was sent to Worcestershire as a missionary and spent the rest of his life in the English Midlands. When he was eventually arrested it was by pure chance. The deputy sheriff and his men were looking for someone else when they raided Rushcock Court, a house near Bromsgrove, where John was staying.

During a five-month imprisonment at Worcester Castle he wrote an account of his sufferings. "Imprisonment in our times, especially when none can send to his friends, nor friends come to him, is the best means to teach us how to put our confidence in God alone in all things," he declared.

Three of the witnesses at his trial were compelled to give evidence by subpoena. Only one testified voluntarily. When he was sentenced, he replied, "Thanks be to God, God save the king, and I beseech God to bless your lordship and all this honorable bench."

"You have spoken very well," replied the judge. "I do not intend that you shall die, at least not for the present, until I know the king's further pleasure."

John was totally sincere in his thanks. As he himself wrote afterwards, "I was not, I thank God for it, troubled with any disturbing thoughts, either against the judge for his sentence, or the jury that gave in such a verdict, or against any of the witnesses . . . esteeming them the best friends to me, in all they did or said, that ever I had in my life."

The judge plainly hoped that John would be reprieved, and he was not the only one. After the court had risen several Protestants, all of them strangers, came to say how sorry they were for him. "To whom with thanks I replied," says John, "that I was troubled they should grieve for me or my condition, who was joyful for it myself."

While under sentence John Wall was taken to London to be cross-examined by Titus Oates himself. Several of the perjurer's henchmen assisted at the interrogation and John's humility and charm obviously affected one of them, a former confidence trickster and jailbird named William Bedloe. Rogue though he was, Bedloe genuinely wanted to save John's life and begged him to conform to the state religion. Both Bedloe and Oates had conceded that John could not have been involved in any plot. If he were to be hanged, he would be hanged for his priesthood and for that alone.

The hoped for reprieve never came. On August 22, 1679, John was taken to the top of Redhill, overlooking the city of Worcester, and hanged. Not long before, he wrote to a friend, "This is the last persecution that will be in England; therefore I hope God will give all his holy grace to make the best use of it."

Five years later Thomas Milward, his Protestant rescuer, was received into the Catholic Church.

On the day that John Wall died another priest suffered the same fate on Widemarsh Common, outside the city of Hereford. His name was John Kemble and he was 80 years old.

A local man, ordained at Douai, he had worked in the area for more than half a century and had already

celebrated his golden jubilee when the new wave of
terror broke out. From his base in Pembridge Castle
he founded mission centers on both sides of the Welsh
border. The ruins of one of these chapels can still be
seen on a hill above Skenfrith.

When friends warned him to hide from the priest
catchers, the old man shook his head. "According to
the course of nature I have but a few years to live," he
said. "It will be an advantage to suffer for my religion
and therefore I will not abscond."

In November, 1678, a squad of men arrived at
Pembridge Castle to arrest John Kemble on suspicion
of being implicated in the "plot". At the head of
these worthies was a Captain Scudamore, whose wife
and children were Catholics and had John for their
pastor.

In Hereford jail he was visited by the Scudamore
children, whom he entertained with food and sweets
sent in to him by friends outside. Asked why, he replied, "Because their father was the best friend I had
in the world."

Despite his age John Kemble was forced, like John
Wall, to ride to London for interrogation by Oates and
his men. By now he was far from well and he suffered
terribly on the journey, the more so because he was
unable to sit astride the horse. Of course the interrogation produced not a shred of evidence against him.
The very suggestion that John could have been a party
to the plot, even had there been one, must have
seemed ridiculous to all but crazed fanatics.

On the morning of his execution the under-sheriff,
whose name was Digges, arrived at the jail and
warned him to make ready. John first asked if he might
finish his prayers and was allowed to do so. Then he
asked if he might smoke a last pipe.

Not only did Digges grant this request, he lit his

own pipe, produced some wine and sat down to keep John company! The episode, so typically English, passed into folklore. Ever afterwards, in the inns of Herefordshire, the last pipe of the evening was called "the Kemble pipe."

Drawn on a hurdle to the common, John did not disappoint the crowd who were awaiting his farewell.

"It will be expected that I should say something," he told them, "but as I am an old man it cannot be much, not having any concern in the plot, neither indeed believing that there is any. Oates and Bedloe not being able to charge me with anything when I was brought up to London, though they were with me, makes it evident that I die only for professing the old Roman Catholic religion, which was the religion that first made this kingdom Christian."

His few words ended, John turned to the hangman, an old friend, and saw that he was deeply distressed. Taking him by the hand, he told him gently, "Honest Anthony, my friend Anthony, be not afraid; do thy office. I forgive thee with all my heart, thou wilt do me a greater kindness than discourtesy."

When the butchery was over, John's nephew begged his body from the authorities and gave it a decent burial in Welsh Newston churchyard. The rope which had hanged him, also kept by his friends, was said to have cured Captain Scudamore's daughter of a serious throat infection, possibly diphtheria.

The attic where he said Mass can be see in Pembridge Castle, now a farm, and his altar is preserved in the Catholic church at Monmouth.

Of the fanatics who seized their chance during the Titus Oates terror, none was more hate-filled than Dorothy James. Why she hated David Lewis so bitterly, we shall never know, but hate him she did. She would never rest, she swore, "until she had washed her hands in his heart's blood and made pottage of his head, as of a sheep's head." Perhaps the unhappy woman was mentally disturbed.

When the terror broke, David and his colleagues went underground. For more than 30 years he had worked among the Catholics of South Wales. To them he was *Tad y Tlodion*, the Father of the poor, because of his generosity to anyone in need. Dorothy and her husband, both renegade Catholics, set themselves to betray him, and in the end they succeeded.

David was about to say Mass in a secret chapel when six dragoons arrived and took him to Abergavenny. From there he was comitted to Monmouth jail, where he was charged 14 shillings a week for his lodging.

For David Lewis, Monmouthshire was home. He had been born there in 1616, one of a family of nine children who were all raised as Catholics save David himself. We do not know precisely how this came about, but we do know that after three months in London studying law, he went to France to work as a tutor and there entered the Catholic Church.

Ordained at Douai, he entered the Society of Jesus soon afterwards and was sent home to Wales at the age of 32. His base was a large farmhouse at the Coombe, an obscure hamlet on the borders of Hereford and Monmouthshire. It was owned by the Jesuits, who named it the College of St. Francis Xavier, a shelter for hunted priests for more than 50 years.

Even before he was caught, Dorothy James had publicly accused him of extorting money to free her father's soul from purgatory, a charge which David indignantly denied. After he had been sentenced he, too, had to face Titus Oates, who tried to link him with the death of Sir Edmund Godfrey, even though he had been 200 miles away at the time.

A court document, still in existence, plainly states the real reason for David's condemnation:

> "An indictment of high treason preferred against him for that he, being born in England, took orders as a seminary priest from the See of Rome, and afterwards came into this county of Monmouth and officiated several times as a popish priest."

Sentenced in March, 1679, David Lewis was not executed until August 27 of that year, one week after John Wall and John Kemble. The gallows had been set up at Usk, on a spot opposite to the site where the town's Catholic church now stands. In his speech to the crowd, we can plainly hear the Welsh lilt:

> "Here is a numerous assembly—may the great Savior of the world save every soul of you all. I believe you are here met not only to see a fellow native die, but also to hear a dying fellow native speak.
>
> "My religion is the Roman Catholic; in it I have lived above these 40 years; in it I now die, and so fixedly die, that if all the good things in this world were offered me to renounce it, all should not remove me one hair's-breadth from my Roman Catholic faith.
>
> "A Roman Catholic I am; a Roman Catholic priest I am; a Roman Catholic priest of that Religious Order called the Society of Jesus I am; and I bless God who first called me.
>
> "Please now to observe: I was condemned for reading Mass, hearing confessions, and administering the sacraments. . . . Dying for this, I die for religion."

Having made this point, he addressed a few words especially to the Catholics who were present:

> "Friends, fear God, honor your king; be firm in your faith, avoid mortal sin by frequenting the sacraments of Holy Church; bear patiently your afflictions and persecutions; forgive your enemies."

So moved by his words were the crowd that they threatened to stone the hangman, a convict who had taken on the task in return for his liberty. The man fled in terror and a blacksmith was bribed to take his place. He carried out the hanging—and never again found work at his own trade.

The reign of Titus Oates, terrible though it was, did not last long. In the end, he overreached himself.

At the trial of Sir George Wakeman he accused not only the physician, but the queen herself, of being implicated in the plot to kill the king. Under searching cross-examination he began to falter and to contradict himself. Before long his story had become so confused and unlikely that he was forced to retire from the witness box on the pretext that he was unwell.

In February, 1681, a priest named Father Atwood, condemned on evidence which Oates had manufactured, was granted a reprieve from the death sentence. Soon afterwards Oates brought a libel action against a man who had openly called him a perjurer. It was dismissed.

As his credibility crumbled, his pension was reduced—a curiously half-hearted measure which showed how reluctant the authorities were to admit, perhaps even to themselves, that Oates was a villain whose lies had hoodwinked them and most of the nation.

On March 10, 1684, Titus Oates appeared in court accused of having called the duke of York a traitor. He was ordered to pay 100,000 pounds damages, an astronomical sum even by today's values.

Thrown into prison and loaded with chains, the perjurer was sentenced to be flogged twice through the streets of London. Bellowing with pain, he was dragged along behind a cart while the whip strokes reduced his back to a bleeding pulp. He barely escaped from the ordeal with his life.

During the Protestant reign of William and Mary, Oates was rehabilitated and was, incredibly, once again granted a small pension, even though his wickedness had been abundantly proved. He never regained any of his former status, however, and the rest of his life was spent in poverty. When he died, in 1705, the public had forgotten him almost entirely.

Bibliography

Butler's Lives of the Saints, edited by Herbert Thurston, S.J., and Donald Attwater (Burns & Oates, London, 1956).

Dictionary of National Biography (Oxford University Press, 1950).

Encyclopedia Brittanica (Chicago, 1973).

History of England, by J.A. Froude (Parker, London, 1858).

Henry VIII and the English Monasteries, by Francis Aidan, Cardinal Gasquet (Hodges, London 1885).

Unpublished Documents Relating to the English Martyrs (Catholic Record Society, London, 1908).

The Religious Orders in England, by David Knowles (Cambridge University Press, 1971).

The English Jesuits, by Bernard Bassett, S.J. (Burns & Oates, London, 1967).

Memoirs of Missionary Priests, by Bishop Challoner (Burns, Oates & Washbourne, London, 1924).

'Vhile the World Revolves, by D.B. Christie (Burns, Oates & Washbourne, London, 1932).

Saints Who Spoke English, by Leo Knowles (Carillon Books, St. Paul, 1979).

Henry VIII, by J.J. Scarisbrick (Eyre and Spottiswood, London, 1968).

Forty Martyrs of England and Wales, by Clement Tigar, S.J. (Stella Maris, Osterley, England, 1961).

A Catholic Dictionary, by William E. Addis and others (Routledge, Kegan Paul, London, 1960).

The Troubles of Our Catholic Forefathers, by John Morris, S.J. (Burns & Oates, London, 1872).

The English Martyrs, by Bede Camm, O.S.B. (Heffer, Cambridge, 1929).

Nine Martyr Monks, by Bede Camm, O.S.B. (Burns, Oates & Washbourne, London, 1931).

The Catholic Martyrs of Wales, by T.P. Ellis (Burns, Oates & Washbourne, London, 1933).

Elizabeth: A Study in Power and Intellect, by Paul Johnson (Weidenfeld & Nicholson, London, 1974).

Lord Burghley and Queen Elizabeth, by Conyers Read (Jonathan Cape, London, 1960).

Forty Martyrs of England and Wales, by James Walsh, S.J. (Catholic Truth Society, London, 1972).

The Life of Robert Southwell, by Christopher Devlin, S.J. (Longman's Green, London, 1956).

The New Oxford Book of English Verse, edited by Helen Gardner (Clarendon Press, Oxford, 1972).

Ambrose Barlow, the Martyr Monk of Manchester, by Justin McCann, O.S.B. (Salford Diocesan Catholic Truth Society, undated).

Henry Morse, Priest of the Plague, by Philip Caraman, S.J. (Longman's Green, London, 1957).

John Gerard, Autobiography of an Elizabethan, translated by Philip Caraman, S.J. (Longman's Green, London, 1965).